Measuring and Marking Metals

Ivan Law

NEXUS SPECIAL INTERESTS

Nexus Special Interests Ltd
Nexus House
Boundary Way
Hemel Hempstead
Herts. HP2 7ST
England

First published 1985
© Argus Books Ltd. 1985
Reprinted 1988, 1990, 1994, 1997

ISBN 0 85242 841 3

Photoset by Manor Typesetting, Broughton, Milton Keynes.
Printed and bound in Great Britain
by Biddles Ltd, Guildford and King's Lynn

Contents

Preface

There are many books written on the subject of measuring and marking-out practice but almost all of them are for the engineering student or professional engineer. They assume that a well-organised workshop is available and it contains all the necessary equipment to accomplish the successful conclusion of any exercise. This book is not written for these people although it is hoped they might find something of interest in it for them. It is primarily intended as a guide to the man who wishes to produce workpieces with limited equipment. This may not only be the model engineer working away in his garden workshop but may also apply to the ever-growing number of jobbing handymen undertaking 'one-off' or prototype work that is of no interest to the larger engineering concerns.

A visit to any model engineering or craft exhibition will show that the amateur, with his basic and sometimes primitive equipment, can produce magnificent examples of engineering craft, demonstrating that it is not the tools that matter but how they are used. It is hoped that this book will not only point the way but may also help the tyro to choose tools that will best serve his purpose.

Eckington 1985.   I.R.L.

Acknowledgements

The author would like to thank Ken Hawley of K. W. HAWLEY (TOOLS) LTD of Sheffield for lending where necessary new tools for photographic purposes. Secondly, he would like to thank G. W. Wainwright who is responsible for almost all of the photographs that appear in this book. Mr. Wainwright went to considerable pains to obtain photographs that illustrated the point the author wished to emphasise.

CHAPTER 1

Concepts of Measurement

Every time we go into our workshop to produce even the smallest component, or part of a component, we have to do some form of measurement. It may be a complicated exercise requiring some form of sophisticated equipment, or it may be a mundane task calling for nothing more than an ordinary rule; occasionally judgment of the eye will be all that is needed, but consciously, or unconsciously, we will be performing some act of measuring.

There are a number of books available on the science of measurement, or, to give it its correct name, metrology, but these are basically for industry rather than the model engineer or home machinist. The needs of the 'back garden' engineer are totally different from those in industry and it is hoped that the following chapters will help to satisfy some of the needs.

The model engineer produces his workpieces with very little equipment and often without the knowledge possessed by a skilled craftsman. It is a case of using his equipment to the best advantage and selecting new tools with care and thought when financial circumstances allow. For it must not be forgotten that expenditure on one's hobby has to come after all other family commitments are met. It is possible that the products of the model engineer's

workshop can equal, and in some cases, surpass, those produced in industry but nevertheless there is one great difference between the home constructor and industry. The model engineer produces all the various components of any mechanism himself with the whole of the project being done in the one workshop, by the same pair of hands, and using the same measuring equipment for all the components.

This fact completely changes the whole concept of measurement. For example, consider the simple cylinder and its piston. In industry the designer or draughtsman would have to consider the maximum and minimum clearance that could be allowed for the correct functioning of the component. Suppose it was decided that the minimum clearance was to be .0005in. and the maximum .0015in. with the nominal size $1\frac{1}{2}$in. The cylinder bore would have to be produced to a size of 1.500in. minimum and 1.5005in. maximum. The piston drawing would call for a maximum of 1.4995in. and a minimum size of 1.499in. In other words the complete tolerance band on each item would be no more than a half of one-thousandth of an inch! Tolerances of this magnitude are expensive to achieve and also difficult to maintain as there is little room for tool wear.

In modern industry it could well be that the two items could be produced in two different and independent factories – indeed, they may even be in two different countries and made by people speaking different languages. The assembly of the items could well be in a third factory completely remote from the other two. It is therefore essential that some very accurate measuring equipment is used by both manufacturing companies and that their respective equipment is set to the same standards. The manufacturing companies must therefore know the actual size of each component. Even when the components are made to these exacting conditions the complete tolerance band of $1\frac{1}{2}$ thousandths of an inch will be frequently experienced. It is not a feasible proposition to give the manufacturers more latitude by increasing the tolerance band by even one half thousandth of an inch in the 'metal on' direction. If this were to be done then "Dr. Sod's" law would most certainly operate and tolerances would accumulate unidirectionally towards maximum difficulty of assembly, the result being that the piston would be an interference fit in the cylinder bore, thus making assembly impossible. The parts would be useless for the purpose for which they were intended and the assembly shop would come to a halt. The whole idea behind the tolerance band, and the expense that the process demands, is to guarantee that any two parts will fit together and give the correct working clearance. There is a system in industry known as selective assembly but this is not used if it can be avoided as selecting parts to obtain a desired fit is clearly time consuming, messy and expensive.

The model engineer's approach to machining and fitting a cylinder and piston is completely nominal. The success of the engine is not dependent on the bore being precisely 1.500in.; it is much more important that the model engineer obtains a round and parallel bore and it is much easier to obtain this condition if the final size is relatively unimportant. The model engineer therefore concentrates his attention not on the size but on the finish. As long as the final size is reasonably near the nominal and is not so large as to interfere with other factors – such as fixing bolts for the cover, or the port and passage ways – the actual size is of no consequence. What does matter is that the piston is made to suit. Since the modeller is making only one, or maybe two, cylinders, interchangeability does not enter into it. Each respective piston is made to fit its own cylinder and will never be required to fit any other.

When the piston is being made no accurate measuring equipment will be required as the cylinder itself will be the final gauge as to size. The constructor may not know, and indeed has no need to know, what the exact sizes are, but he will be able to obtain a nice sliding fit and in all probability, a closer one than the $1\frac{1}{2}$-thou obtained by his industrial counterpart. This condition will have been achieved without the expensive and sophisticated measuring equipment used in industry. In fact the only measuring tool the modeller may have used might be an ordinary steel rule. To assist in getting the piston near to its final size an outside micrometer may have been used, the procedure being to set a pair of inside calipers to the cylinder bore, adjusting the micrometer to the caliper size and then using the micrometer to turn the piston nearly to size. Even if this method has been used the final fitting will have been obtained by using the cylinder as the gauge.

The model engineer will have used his

equipment not to measure the actual size but as comparators — and that is, as the word suggests, to compare one size to another one. When used in this way the measuring equipment need not be accurate to British Standard Institute requirements, indeed it could well be inaccurate, but as its duty is to transfer a size from one component onto another, the inaccuracy is of no consequence. Quite often when using measuring equipment as comparators the units shown on the equipment are of no consequence. They could be imperial, metric or even millifurlongs, it matters not! Bowlers on the bowling greens use a piece of string to compare two bowls to the jack. This measure has no unit calibrated on it at all, yet the nearest bowl to the jack can be ascertained to within close limits!

Only one example has been discussed above but the same principle applies to almost the whole of modelmaking: the desired fit between components can be achieved by producing one component to a 'nominal' size and producing its mating part to fit. It can therefore be realised that the whole concept of measurement in model engineering is completely different from general production practice. This is fortunate as far as we modellers are concerned since it means that we do not have to purchase a large amount of measuring equipment, nor do we have to have it constantly checked in order to maintain its accuracy. I have heard people claim that they can measure with a steel rule to within .002in.; they can't, of course, as this is less than the tolerances allowed by the manufacturers of the rules between any two marks. They can, perhaps, if they have good eyesight or use a magnifying glass, compare two sizes to within .002in. using the same rule, but this is not measuring, this is another example of using a rule as a comparator.

As can be seen from the above, any beginner to the model engineering hobby need have no fears at all about his ability to produce parts to the linear standards required. He will be able to construct a perfectly satisfactory working model using simple measuring equipment provided he uses it intelligently and understands just what it is that he is trying to achieve. The man the beginner has to ignore is the chap who, at club meetings, announces that whatever component he is making he always measures to a "tenth of a thou". Maybe he does, but it is doubtful if he knows which one! — fortunately it rarely matters.

CHAPTER 2

Rules and Calipers

RULES

The most common, and certainly the best-known, piece of measuring equipment is the ordinary rule. In actual fact, after looking into the number and types of rules available, the term 'ordinary rule' becomes meaningless. There is a large number of types and styles of rules available, most trades and crafts having their own special rules or range of rules. However, all these can be disregarded; as far as the model or amateur engineer is concerned the term 'rule' means what the trade calls "Engineers' precision steel rule". Even when the field is narrowed down to this small band, there is still a number of rules left from which a choice can be made.

The model engineer rarely requires a rule above twelve inches long even though a model may be large, like a 5in. gauge locomotive, as it is very rare to find that any feature is more than twelve inches from a given datum. We can say, therefore, that for marking-out purposes we require a 12in. rule or, if the model is metric-based, the equivalent size rule of 300 mm. We have a few from which we can make our selection. A rule can have one end square – this being the end from which all measurements are to be made

and from which all the graduations are based – and the other end rounded with the graduations ending about a half-inch or so from this rounded end. A small hole is usually drilled in this plain portion, thus providing a means of hanging it onto a hook on the wall or drawer cabinet when not in use. This type of rule is known by manufacturers as a 'round-end rule'.

Another type of rule is called the 'square-end rule', and this, as its name suggests, is square at both ends and as a result either end can be used as the datum end when measuring. With this type a 12in. rule is, within the limits of manufacture, exactly twelve inches long. The method of graduating differs from the round-end rule in that, with the round-end rule, when this is held so that the rounded end is to the right, both scales – top and bottom – are of necessity graduated from the square or left-hand end, and both scales have to be read with the rule held in this attitude otherwise the graduations and numbers are upside down. With the square-ended rule the graduations are arranged so that no matter how the rule is held the markings always start from the left-hand end, so that when held in the hand the bottom edge, or the one nearest to the user, is the one to be read. It is not

Fig.1 This shows four different styles of 12-inch or 300mm rules. The top two are round-end rules, the lower two are square-ended. The upper one is a two-edge rule whilst the other three are the four-edged variety.

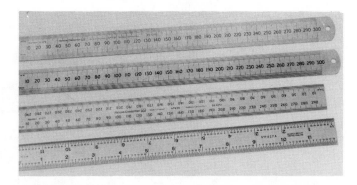

possible to say that one type is better or more useful than the other, for if this were so only one type would be made. Both types have advantages and disadvantages. If the workshop had to be limited to only one 12in. rule then the author would prefer the square-ended type but, if possible, it is an advantage to have one example of each type. Figs. 1 and 2 illustrate four 12in. or 300mm rules.

The 12in. or 300 mm rule is, however, rather large for measuring workpieces held in the relatively small machine tools found in the home workshop and for this type of work the 6in. or 150 mm rule is decidedly superior. For example, it is difficult to apply the 12in. rule to a workpiece in the lathe without moving the tailstock from its supporting position and sliding it down towards the end of the bed to allow access for the rule. It is both quicker and easier to use the 6in. rule in this and similar circumstances.

Like the 12in. rule, the 6in. rule is made in both rounded-and square-ended styles. The same method and pattern of markings are used on the small rules as on the larger ones. There is, however, one big difference between them and that is in the width of the two rules, the 12in. and 300 mm rules are supplied with a width of 1in. or 25 mm, while the smaller rules are usually 3/4in. or 19 mm wide.

All the rules described above are of the

Fig.2 This shows the reverse side of the same four rules. As can be seen, the two-edge rule has no markings on it at all. The second rule down is imperial on this side and therefore has two metric edges and two imperial edges. The upper square-ended rule has four metric edges whilst the lower one has two imperial edges.

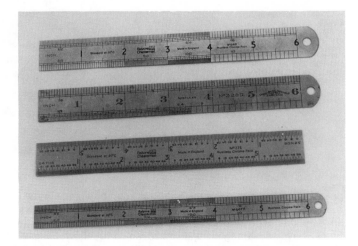

Fig.3 This illustration shows four six-inch or 150mm rules. The top three are rigid rules whilst the lower one is flexible.Three are round-edge rules and one is square-ended. The second one down is a bright finish rule whilst the others have a non-reflecting pearl chrome finish.

type known as rigid; this means that they do not bend easily and they should be kept and used in the 'flat' state in which they are supplied. There is available, however, another type of rule known as the flexible steel rule which is much thinner and narrower than the rigid rule and made from spring steel. The flexible rules, both 12in. and 6in. long (or metric equivalent) are usually only $\frac{1}{2}$in. wide and this, and the fact that they are manufactured from thinner material allows them to bend to an extent far greater than would be required in normal use, and without taking on a permanent set or breaking. Again, this range of rules is available round-ended or square-ended and a 6in. square-ended rule of this type is very useful for measuring workpieces held in the lathe as both its size and flexibility allow it to be used in spaces that would make direct measurement with other rules difficult, if not impossible.

Rules made with graduations on one

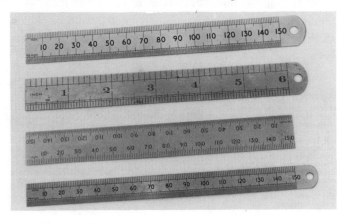

Fig.4 The reverse side of the 'six-inch' rules. The bright-finish rule has four imperial edges whilst the others have two imperial and two metric edges. It is unusual for a square-ended rule to have both imperial and metric edges as the length of the two scales is not similar and as a result the top and bottom scales on one are out of register. This can be seen on the metric scales on the square-ended rule.

12

Fig.5 This photograph shows the advantage of the flexible rule when measuring in the lathe. It is possible to obtain a reading without withdrawing the tailstock support by 'bending' the rule to lay on the workpiece.

side and plain on the other are termed 'two-edge rules'. The other, and more common, rules are the four-edge rules and, as its name implies, this rule has graduations on both sides thus allowing all four edges to be utilized. As can be imagined there are many ways and permutations that can be employed on graduating rules. The all-imperial four-edge can be obtained with the scale in 1/32in. and 1/64in. on one side whilst the reverse side has 1/8in. and 1/16in. spacings. There are some imperial rules that have scales graduated in 1/10in. – 1/20in. with short lengths – usually one-inch – marked 1/50in. and 1/100in.

Fig.6 Using the same rule to set the position of a parting tool. Note, a different edge is being used than in the previous illustration. This is possible because with a round-ended rule both scales have the same datum end. This type of rule is very useful for measuring workpieces in the lathe.

respectively. The author finds that fine graduations such as 1/64in. and 1/100in. are too fine for the naked eye and difficult to read; it can be easier to judge to 1/64in. by using the 1/32in. scale rather than the 1/64in. range which is difficult to see clearly.

One advantage of the metric scale is that it eliminates the necessity for a range of fractional sizes. The markings on a metric rule are every millimetre or half-millimetre with the figures marked at 10 mm intervals. Some rules are dual marked with both metric and imperial scales on the one rule; there are examples with two-edge imperial on one side and two-edge metric on the other whilst other rules may have metric and imperial on the same side. The whole range of rules can be obtained in either carbon steel or rustless steel with either a bright finish or a non-reflecting pearl chrome finish. The modern trend is towards the non-reflecting finish as not only does this eliminate glare but it also makes for bolder markings.

If the modeller wishes to have a longer rule then both the two-edge and the four-edge rigid steel rule can be obtained in 24in., 36in. and also one metre lengths but, as previously mentioned, these long rules would not be in regular use. It is not practical to use a long rule when measuring small distances as the long length not being used waves about and gets in the way and will almost certainly foul something, particularly in the small back-garden workshop.

There is also a type of rule known as a folding rule. This rule is pivoted in one or more places along its length and, as its name suggests, folds over itself so that when not in use and folded, it is only a half, or in some cases one quarter, of its extended length. If the modeller possesses a rule of this type it is not recommended that it be used for serious work but rather that it is the one to lend to his wife when she wishes to measure the length of her knitting!

It can be seen from the above that there is a large range of rules to choose from and it is not possible to state categorically which is the best for model engineering – it all depends on the individual modeller. However, if the home workshop is equipped with a 12in. or 300mm rigid rule, a 6in. or 150mm rigid rule and a 6in. or 150mm flexible rule then it should be capable of meeting all the demands made upon it, at least as far as rule measurement is concerned.

CALIPERS

These tools are purely and simply comparators, used for transferring a dimension from one place to another. The transfer is usually from the rule or micrometer to the workpiece but, in the case of two mating components, the comparison is between one finished component to the mating piece under construction. It is often thought that calipers are not precision tools and are only used where the work does not call for a high degree of accuracy. This is not necessarily the case; even in a well-equipped model engineer's workshop, where micrometers are available for measuring outside diameters, inside diameters such as holes may have to be gauged be means of inside calipers. Even supposing inside micrometers are available, the majority of holes produced by the model engineer will be too small to allow the inside micrometer to enter. There are other ways of gauging these holes but as these alternatives require special equipment, calipers may have to be used. An experienced craftsman can detect a difference of a half-thou using inside calipers and even the amateur, with a little practice, should soon be able to

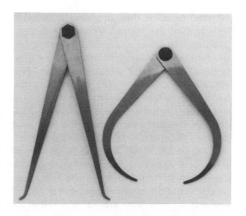

Fig.7 This shows a pair of inside and a pair of outside firm-joint calipers.

develop a sense of touch which will enable him to detect a difference of one-thousandth of an inch provided that the calipers are set and used correctly.

Calipers are made in two distinct types, those used for gauging holes and those used for 'outside' features such as shafts, etc. They are naturally termed 'inside' and 'outside' calipers respectively. The two legs of the inside variety are straight and tapered with the ends curving out to provide small 'feet'. These feet should be rounded and have all sharp edges removed, thus allowing them to move over the workpiece smoothly, so eliminating the possibility of a false reading. The legs of outside calipers are bowed, which is to allow them to provide clearance when passing over the workpiece. Both types of caliper are made in either 'firm joint' or spring type. The firm joint is the simplest pattern, the two legs being held together and pivoted by means of a large-headed nut and screw. A thin fibre washer is interposed between the contacting faces to provide a firm and rigid joint which will also allow a smooth movement free from play.

The spring type have their legs pivoted on a roller and the legs are tensioned by means of a strong bow spring. The adjustment for measuring is made by opening and closing the legs by means of an adjusting nut. The screw on which the adjusting nut rotates is small in diameter and therefore of fine pitch, which allows fine setting to be made by simply turning the nut. This means that to move the legs from the closed position to a wide open-

ing the knurled nut has to be rotated a considerable number of times which can be frustrating and lead to a sore thumb and first finger if the operation has to be performed a number of times. To overcome this problem calipers with a quick-acting nut can be obtained. This nut is designed and made in two halves, the two halves being kept together by means of a bevelled closing washer or cone and held in place by the pressure of the spring. When the two caliper legs are squeezed together by the fingers, pressure on the closing cone is released and the nut is

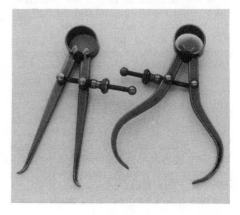

Fig.8 The spring-bow calipers shown here are far more popular than the firm-joint type, particularly in the smaller size. The author, however, prefers the firm-joint type as they give a more positive 'feel' in use.

allowed to open thus enabling it to move rapidly over the thread. When the desired position has been approximately obtained the legs are gradually released, the spring pressure closes the nut and the final fine adjustment can be made by rotating the nut in the normal manner.

Calipers are made in a variety of sizes and commercial examples of the firm joint calipers of both inside and outside pattern can be obtained up to a nominal size of 24in. or 600mm. The largest spring bow pattern at present listed in the manufacturers' catalogue is 12in. or 300mm. Calipers of this size are far too large for our workshop requirements, in fact, our requirements are usually for the smallest sizes available. The size of the calipers is determined by the length of the legs measured from the pivot point to the other ends or 'feet'. Thus, a 3in. caliper has legs three inches long. This nominal size is also the effective range of the caliper, so a 3in. caliper can effectively measure from zero to three inches. If calipers are to be used to obtain a specific size, then no matter how good is the user's 'feel' the deciding factor is how they are set in the first place.

In the modeller's workshop, outside calipers are nearly always set by means of a rule or standard. The word 'standard' here could mean the mating part to the one being measured. When setting to the rule always follow the same procedure or method as many of the inaccuracies obtained by calipers are as a result of incorrect setting and the incorrect setting is due to not using the correct technique. The author, who is right-handed, uses the method outlined below. Left-handed operators could of course follow the same basic procedure but reversing the handing. It is also recommended that left-handed people use a round-ended rule, otherwise the most convenient scale on the rule would be graduated towards zero

rather than away from zero. Hold the rule upright in the left hand – a 6in. rigid is the ideal rule here– with the square end resting on the third finger and the rule supported between the thumb and first two fingers – try to keep your little finger out of the way! The rule should be in the 'North-South' position and tilted to an angle of about 45°, which gives you in effect an "angled vertical" scale on which to place the calipers.

Now, holding the calipers in the right hand, and in the case of the spring type by means of the spring, place one leg of the calipers on the end of the rule, holding the leg in contact with the rule. The third finger of your left hand will steady the caliper leg and form a support for it and will also stop the foot of the caliper leg from falling off the end of the rule. This will ensure that one leg of the caliper is in contact with the zero reading on the rule and we can then give our whole attention to the setting of the other leg. The rule reading will be the caliper setting, there being no need to add bits on or take them off. This may seem a superfluous bit of information but more than one workpiece has been scrapped by the operator using a rule, probably well worn on the end, and to compensate for this, setting his calipers from the one-inch line then forgetting to allow for this! It is unlikely that the amateur would do this as his workpiece is usually small and a one-inch discrepancy would be immediately apparent.

With the spring bow type the movement of the caliper legs is clearly controlled by means of the knurled nut and so very small movement can be easily achieved. If fixed joint type tools are being used then the leg movement is obtained by tapping the limb on a solid object. Which limb is tapped depends on whether the legs are to be opened or closed. Sometimes if a small openig movement is

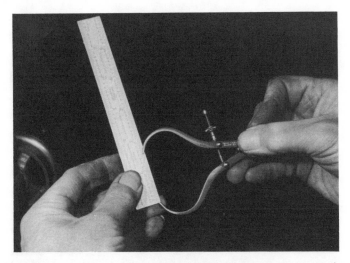

Fig.9 This shows the recommended method of setting outside calipers to a rule. One leg of the caliper is firmly placed on the datum end of the rule, the third finger provides the support and steadies the whole tool.

required the joint can be tapped, which is done by holding the caliper in a vertical position, joint down, and then smartly bringing the instrument down onto a solid object; the resulting 'shock' has the effect of opening the legs slightly. Although this method works it is not really to be recommended as the joint can get burred over and this then affects the smooth working of the instrument.

Setting calipers by the above method, and illustrated in fig. 9, rather than placing them onto the mid-scale of the rule, as in fig. 11, will give a greater degree of accuracy because one leg is always in contact with the datum edge of the rule and

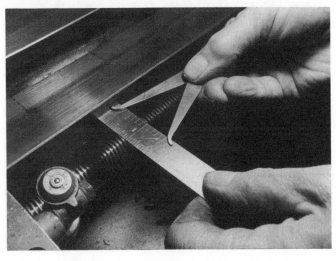

Fig.10 Setting a pair of inside calipers to the rule. Placing both the end of the rule and one leg of the caliper onto a flat face ensures that the caliper leg is coincident with the datum end of the rule.

17

Fig.11 How not to set calipers – a setting error is possible on both legs and neither the rule nor calipers is under complete control.

therefore any error in reading the setting can only occur on the one remaining leg.

Inside calipers are usually used far more frequently than the outside variety in small workshops. This is because for outside work micrometers, if available, are much easier to use and read. They are also quick to set and will give a more accurate reading, particularly in the hands of a relatively inexperienced craftsman. However, as most of the holes produced in the small, or modeller's, workshop will be of small diameters, indeed most will be under one inch or 25mm diameter, some means other than micrometers will have to be used as it is impractical to produce

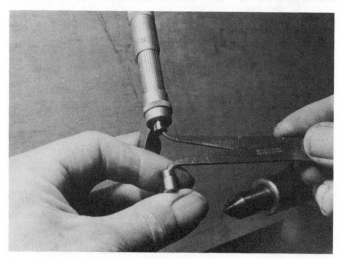

Fig.12 Showing how to set inside calipers to a micrometer. Note that one leg of the calipers is resting on the first finger: this is the pivot point about which the whole caliper is rotated until the correct setting is obtained.

Fig.13 This method of setting inside calipers is not recommended. The operator has very little control and the chances of obtaining a correct setting are, to say the least, hazardous.

micrometers small enough to enter holes of this size. The cheapest and simplest alternative is the inside caliper gauge. As with the outside type, the problem is setting the caliper correctly. For many operations setting to the rule will be satisfactory and, if set and used correctly, the results obtained will be surprisingly accurate.

To get the best results follow the principle suggested when setting the outside gauge of anchoring one leg to a datum and taking the reading from the other leg. To do this some solid flat face must be used. When working in the lathe, such as the ML7-type, the front shear of the bed gives an ideal face for a datum but if the lathe has a dovetail bed some other flat surfaces will be available. This time lay the rule across all four fingers and clamp by means of the thumb – held this way the rule is quite rigid. The square end of the rule can now be pushed firmly up to the flat datum face. Take the calipers in the other hand and hold them by the spring or pivot joint in a similar way as previously described. The calipers are now placed flat on the rule and moved along it until one leg comes into contact with the datum; this leg is now coincident with the end of the rule so a direct reading can now be taken on the other leg. Fig. 10 illustrates a pair of inside calipers being set using this method.

If an outside micrometer is available then use this for setting the inside caliper. Not only are they easier to set but also a much greater degree of accuracy can be achieved than is possible by using a rule. There is also one other great advantage in using the micrometer to set the calipers. The caliper will be set between two faces and as the legs pass between these, a slight resistance or 'feel' will be experienced. If the same 'feel' is used when gauging the workpiece, errors in the size owing to the 'feel' being too heavy will have a tendency to be minimised. Once again it is advisable to develop good habits when setting the calipers to a micrometer. The degree of success obtained when measuring internal diameters is largely dependent on the sense of 'feel' developed by the operator. The caliper is set by 'feeling' between the anvil and spindle of the micrometer, and the hole is

19

gauged by 'feeling' two diametrically opposite points on the bore being measured. Since the micrometer can be set to a high degree of accuracy any errors that arise are, in the main, due to the operator's use of the calipers. However, as previously mentioned, an operator should, with care, be quickly able to develop a technique that enables him to compare to within one-thousandth of an inch or even smaller, provided he follows a sound method of operation.

The method used by the author and illustrated in fig. 12 is as follows. First of all set the micrometer to the size required (micrometer settings are covered in the next chapter) and lock the spindle firmly, which will prevent any movement and consequent alterations in the setting whilst the caliper is being adjusted. Now, hold the micrometer in the left hand with the anvil between the thumb and first finger and with the other three fingers spaced around the back of the frame, thus giving firm support to the tool. The first finger should cover about a half of the an-

vil, this can be seen in the photograph. Now, hold the micrometer with the frame vertically downwards and the spindle nearly horizontal. At the same time hold the calipers in the right hand by means of the spring or joint. If the calipers are held between the thumb and first and second fingers it will be easy and simple to give a twisting or rotary action to the calipers. Next, and this is important, place one caliper leg on the anvil and if the first finger is in the correct place then it will give support and form a platform for the caliper leg to rest on. Now, using this leg as a pivot point rotate the calipers through the gap between the anvil and the spindle. It will be apparent at once whether they need opening or closing. Adjust until the second leg just makes contact as it passes through the gap, this is where the 'feel' is experienced. Contact should only just be made; if force has to be used to get the calipers through the gap then they are oversize. When set correctly the weight of the caliper should be sufficient to allow it to pass between the two contact faces of

Fig.14 Sizing a bore with inside calipers. Note one leg of the caliper is firmly held onto the workpiece, this is the pivot point.

20

the micrometer without any extra force being needed. Most inexperienced users have too heavy a 'feel' – errors as large as five thou can be experienced if the 'feel' is too heavy.

The above may seem complicated to follow but once the technique has been mastered no difficulty should ever be encountered in setting calipers to close limits. Once the calipers are set to size, the workpiece can be checked and, of course, errors can arise here if a sound technique is not used. Fig. 14 shows a bore being gauged. One leg of the calipers is placed in the bore (if accessible the bottom "dead centre" is the best place for this leg) and is then pressed firmly onto the surface of the bore by means of the first finger of the left hand – this provides an anchor or pivot point on which to rotate or swing the caliper. The calipers are again held by the joint using the thumb on one side of the joint and the first and second fingers on the other side. Keeping the bottom leg in place by means of the finger, pivot or swing the calipers about this point; the movement will be in

the vertical plane. If the second leg of the calipers will not enter then the bore is too small, if the calipers will enter and also allow side-to-side movement then the bore is too large. The correct size is when the calipers will pass through the bore at a point diametrically opposite to the anchor point and just touch as it passes through. In fact, the 'feel' should be the same as was experienced between the micrometer and the calipers during the setting operations.

If the bore is oversize then some side-to-side movement of the calipers will be possible, but small side-to-side movement does not mean that the bore is dramatically oversize. A very small amount of clearance between the bore and the calipers results in side-to-side play many times greater than the clearance. For instance, a clearance of .001in. on a one-inch bore will give a side-to-side movement of about 1/16in. If, therefore, a small amount of side-to-side movement is experienced, the component may well be within the permitted tolerance range. When boring to a specific size and that

21

size is being approached it is as well to know just how much material has to be removed so that the cutting tool can be moved the correct amount. In this case the whole process is reversed and the calipers set to the bore and then the micrometer set to the calipers and a reading obtained. But whichever way the operation is carried out the basic principle of holding and setting is the same.

It can be seen that calipers, if used correctly, are very useful tools and in small workshops where cost rules out sophisticated measuring equipment, they are virtually indispensable. The main point to remember is always to anchor one caliper leg and use the other caliper leg to obtain the 'feel'. If both legs are waving about, fine control and a light 'feel' become very difficult, if not impossible, to achieve, fig. 15. This applies equally to both the setting, whether by rule or micrometer, and to the actual use on the component being produced.

CHAPTER 3

Micrometers

The outside micrometer appears very early on the tools list of the amateur who is building up his workshop equipment. As a result of modern methods of manufacture, micrometers are not an expensive luxury, particularly when one considers that they are a precision instrument and are an extremely useful and handy piece of equipment which, once obtained and if handled with card, will last a lifetime. There is, of course, a whole range of micrometers but by far the most useful for the model engineer is the one that covers the range of sizes between zero and one inch. Larger ones, such as the one-to-two inch or the two-to-three inch, can be acquired as the opportunity arises, but the larger ones will get far less use than the zero-to-one inch and the amateur could well be right in thinking that a vernier-type caliper would be of more use for his needs than a range of larger micrometers.

Metric micrometers have an increment range of 25mm steps and so are almost identical in physical size to the imperial ones which are calibrated to read to one-thousandth of an inch. To divide a scale only one inch long into 1,000 parts is obviously impractical so some means must be found of magnifying the graduations. This is achieved by means of a screw

nut, and this is basically what a micrometer is – a screw and a nut, albeit a high precision one! The body of the instrument is the nut into which the screw or spindle fits, and it is the screw that rotates and does the actual measuring. The imperial micrometer screw has a pitch of 40 threads per inch which means that one complete turn of the screw will give a forward or backward movement of 1/40in. or .025in. All that is now required is to divide an attachment to the screw into 25 equally spaced divisions around its circumference and we have an increment of .001in. This attachment, which is called the thimble, is a sort of tubular cover which is fastened onto the outer end of the spindle and therefore moves with the spindle. It is the circumference of this thimble that is divided into 25 equal parts. Every fifth division is numbered, starting from zero, which means that the 25th division coincides with zero and is marked zero. The point to remember is that the zero mark indicates the beginning or end of a full turn. The numbering is arranged to rise as the micrometer is opened.

In the case of metric micrometers, the pitch of the screw is $\frac{1}{2}$mm and the thimble is divided into 50 divisions thus giving an increment of .01mm. Obviously some

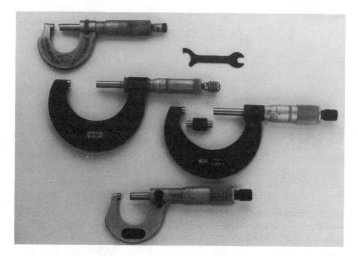

Fig.16 This shows four micrometers: two are 0-1" instruments whilst the other two have a range of 1"to 2". A great many examples of the upper two micrometers were made over a long period of time but this style has now been superseded by the two lower examples. Micrometers over an inch in size are usually provided with a standard, this can be seen in the photograph, which is used in both checking and re-adjusting the instrument,. All four of the micrometers shown here were manufactured by the Sheffield company Moore and Wright.

means of counting the complete number of turns of the thimble must be found and this is done by placing markings on the sleeve, which is an extension to the frame and over which the thimble rotates. In the case of the imperial micrometer, each turn of the thimble advances the screw .025in. therefore four turns will give an advancement of .100in. The markings are so arranged that every fourth mark has a longer line than the intermediate marks and is stamped with a number rising from 0 to 9. In order to make it easier to distinguish the lines, every second one, or each .050in., has a line slightly longer than the .025in. line but not as long as the .100in.

Micrometer readings are always expressed in decimals. All metric measurements are, of course, but with the imperial system the majority of dimensions shown on drawings used in the model or amateur workshop are given in fractions of an inch. In order to use the micrometer these fractions must be converted to decimal equivalents. It used to be the practice for manufacturers to engrave conversion tables on the frame or thimbles of micrometers and these tables gave all decimal equivalents in steps of 1/64in. It would appear from the current pattern of micrometers being produced that this practice is being discontinued. If your instrument is one of this new style then it is advisable to have a conversion chart permanently fastened to the workshop wall for quick reference.

A micrometer reading is a combination of two scales, the sleeve scale and the thimble scale. The sleeve scale indicates just how many turns the thimble has made. As previously discussed, with an imperial micrometer each turn is .025in. and therefore every four turns is 4 × .025in. or .100 inches. The first decimal place of our reading is obtained by reading directly from the sleeve scale. If the '2' mark is visible but not the '3', then the reading is somewhere between .200in. and .300in. Now count the number of lines visible after the number and if we can see three lines but not four, then the second decimal place is greater than 7 because 3 × .025in. is .075in. We now know then that our reading is between .275in. and .300in. To obtain the final increment we look at the thimble and read off the number of lines that have passed the long datum line after the third .025in. division. As the thimble is engraved with the relevant numbers this is a simple matter. If, say, the line marked '16' is coincident with the datum line then we have to add .016in. to our previous figure. The correct reading is therefore .275in. + .016in., or .291in. Fig. 17 shows this reading diagrammatically. Two further examples are also shown, one being a reading of .034in., the other being .463in.

The same principle of reading applies with the metric micrometer inasmuch as there are two scales. The pitch of the spindle thread is .5mm so the scale on the sleeve is in half-millimetres. If the divisions were to be marked every .5mm then these lines would be very close together and confusion could arise. To overcome this the scale is usually split into two. On one side of the sleeve datum line are marked 1mm divisions which are usually

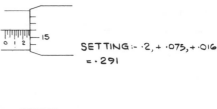

SETTING :- ·2, + ·075, + ·016
= ·291

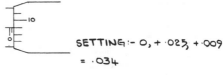

SETTING :- 0, + ·025, + ·009
= ·034

SETTING :- ·400, + ·050,
+ ·013 = ·463

Fig.17 An example of three micrometer settings (imperial).

numbered in groups of five and the thimble has to make two revolutions to move

Fig.18 Showing the sleeve and thimble graduation on a metric micrometer. The reading depicted is 8.20mm.

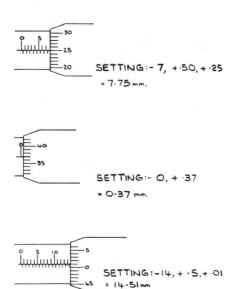

SETTING :- 7, + ·50, + ·25
= 7·75 mm.

SETTING :- 0, + ·37
= 0·37 mm.

SETTING :- 14, + ·5, + ·01
= 14·51 mm

Fig.19 An example of three micrometer settings (metric).

one of these divisions. On the other side of the datum line, and midway between the 1mm divisions, is a scale of shorter lines. It is therefore possible to see at a glance whether the thimble is in the first or second revolution from the last millimetre mark. The thimble is graduated into 50 divisions, which means that the lines are closer together than on the imperial thimble but the thimbles are large enough to give clear marks and no confusion should arise. Fig. 18 shows a metric micrometer and illustrates the graduations.

As the metric micrometer measures in millimetres there is usually a number before the decimal point and only two numbers after the decimal point. The numbers which appear on the sleeve before the thimble covers them over are the numbers of whole millimetres. If seven numbers can be seen then the reading is

between 7mm and 8mm. if one of the small half-lines is uncovered, then the reading is between 7.5mm and 8mm. To complete the reading the number shown on the thimble has to be added on. If this is 25, then the complete reading is 7.5mm + .25mm, or 7.75mm; fig. 19 shows this diagrammatically. Two further examples of metric readings are also depicted. It can be seen from the above that the metric micrometer reads to two places and not three places of decimals as is the case with the imperial version; however, when one considers that a millimetre is less than .040 of an inch it will be appreciated that .01mm is only about 4 ten-thousandths of an inch.

For many years now micrometers have been fitted with two refinements which are a great help to the user. The first of these is the spindle lock which is a device which enables the spindle to be positively locked in any position. The micrometer can be set to a desired position and then locked. This is very useful if the instrument is being used as a gauge for setting calipers or telescopic gauges, etc. If the spindle is not locked then it may inadvertently be moved whilst the micrometer is being withdrawn from the workpiece and a false setting obtained. Also, if a number of components are to be checked then the micrometer can be set to the size required, locked in position and then used as a fixed gauge. For many years this locking was obtained by means of a knurled nut working in a slot in the frame but Moore & Wrights of Sheffield, who are one of the leading manufacturers of micrometrs, have replaced the knurled ring with a small lever. Fig. 16 shows examples of both types.

The second refinement is the ratchet stop and this is a device placed on the end of the thimble. A 40 t.p.i. screw is a fine thread and only a relatively slight pressure on the thimble can result in a considerable force being exerted between the two anvils. If the force were to be excessive then it would be possible to overstress the frame thus causing permanent damage to the micrometer which would in turn lead to incorrect readings being obtained. Even amongst more experienced users it is possible for 'touch' to vary and this can lead to two people obtaining slightly different results from the same micrometer and workpiece. There is a tendency, especially amongst inexperienced operators, to have a heavy touch. To overcome this problem the ratchet stop is fitted and this drives the thimble through a ratchet device. This ratchet will always 'slip' at the same pressure and so uniform readings can be obtained. It also protects the micrometer frame from being overstressed and so helps prevent distortion due to heavy-handed operators.

It is a good idea for an inexperienced operator to measure an article using the ratchet then measure the same article without the ratchet. This will show him if his touch is heavy or not. If he goes on measuring different items both with and without the ratchet he will quickly develop a good sense of touch. In the home workshop, where all measuring is done by the same person using the same equipment, a sense of touch slightly heavier or lighter than the ratchet is of little importance as any errors will have a tendency to be cancelled out because any mating component will be subjected to the same touch. A micrometer used in thse conditions is really being employed as a comparator.

Micrometers are precision instruments and should be treated as such; with care they will last the amateur a lifetime but, like any other engineering device, they not only need careful handling but also servicing. Taking care of them is a matter of common sense; do not leave them lying about on the bench otherwise they may easily get knocked onto the floor and this could cause damage and upset their accuracy, again resulting in incorrect readings. Micrometers are supplied in a box or case and it is a good idea to keep this box open on the bench and always to return the micrometer to the box after use. Before putting the micrometer away wipe it over carefully to remove any foreign matter and if it is not going to be used again for some time, apply a thin coat of good quality non-corrosive oil onto the measuring faces and bright areas. The manufacturers recommend a lanolin-based oil as being the most suitable but any light machine oil will be suitable for this purpose.

When in use always see that the anvil faces are clean, as the merest suspicion of dirt or oil can result in a false reading. To clean the faces on the type of micrometer where the anvils meet, such as the 0-1in. or 0-25mm, open the anvil and spindle faces slightly and insert a piece of paper between them, then close the faces so that the paper is lightly gripped, then withdraw the paper by sliding it out. Any dirt or grease will be removed and even if you think that the face is clean it will be surprising how dirty the cleaning paper becomes! If the micrometer is one of the larger type where the anvils do not meet then give them a good clean with some absorbent paper.

The best way to hold a micrometer in order to use it will depend both on the size of the micrometer and also on the location or position of the workpiece. If the workpiece is relatively small and has to be held in the hand then only one hand will be

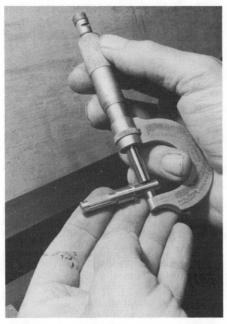

Fig.20 This shows one way of holding a micrometer for sizing a small workpiece. This is a comfortable and easy method but it does not permit free use of the ratchet.

micrometer in the right hand. Owing to the nature of the workpiece the micrometer will probably be one of the smallest, or 0-1in. range. This size can be comfortably held and used in one hand. Hold it so that the thumb and first finger can rotate the thimble, the second finger steadies the thimble or barrel, whilst the third finger is passed through the frame and holds it in the palm of the hand. Fig. 20 shows a micrometer being used this way. Held in this way excellent control of both workpiece and instrument is obtained but it does have one drawback – it is not easy to operate the ratchet. The author, who for many years used micrometers without the refinement of a ratchet, still prefers this method even though his workshop is now equipped with modern micrometers.

available for both holding and operating the tool. In this case, one way is to hold the workpiece in the left hand and the

If the operator wishes to use the ratchet then the technique will have to be changed. Hold the micrometer in the left hand this time, the frame resting on all

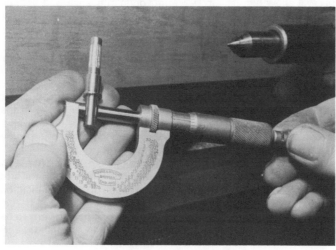

Fig.21 An alternative method of holding the micrometer which does allow for full use to be made of the ratchet.

28

four fingers and clamped by the thumb. The workpiece is now placed between the anvil and also lies across the fingers and is supported by the thumb. The right hand is now free to rotate the ratchet and a reading can be obtained. Fig. 21 shows this operation being performed.

If the workpiece is still in the lathe, or any other machine, then it will be securely held and both hands will be free to operate the mcirometer. In this case hold the micrometer in the right hand with all four fingers around the back edge of the frame and the thumb on the inside of the frame clamping it onto the four fingers. The micrometer is thus securely held, but under full control; hold it with the spindle and thimble in the vertical position. Now, with the anvil faces opened to a size greater than the workpiece, bring the micrometer over the workpiece and operate the thimble or ratchet with the left hand. Fig. 22 shows this operation being carried out. The micrometer will have to be withdrawn from the workpiece in order for the operator to see and read the engravings. There is a possibility that the thimble might get moved a small amount during this withdrawing operation and this would of course give rise to a false reading. After the anvils have closed onto the workpiece there is in fact no need for the thimble to be touched at all before the reading is taken. If this rule is followed then no trouble should be experienced with false readings. In order to check the reading obtained, clamp the spindle by means of the spindle lock and try the micrometer over the workpiece again, when it will be apparent at once if any movement has taken place.

There is one golden rule that must be followed in all cases when using a micrometer and this is to keep the anvils or measuring faces square with the object being measured. If this rule is not followed the corners of the anvil will be in contact with the workpiece and not the flat surface and the result will be an incorrect reading. If, however, the micrometer is held in the ways outlined above, and as shown in the illustrations, this problem is unlikely to arise as the measuring faces will automatically pull the micrometer

Fig.22 Showing how to hold the micrometer for measuring a workpiece still held in the lathe. The micrometer should be securely held but not too firmly otherwise an incorrect gauging could arise owing to the anvils not being square to the surface of the workpiece.

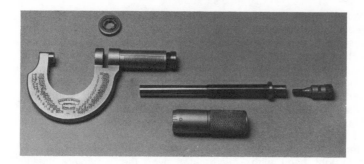

Fig.23 A 0-1" micrometer dismantled for cleaning. The three components of the locking ring are shown assembled.

square as the thimble is turned and although the micrometer is securely held, it is not firmly or rigidly held, so it will be free to move into the correct position.

Micrometers are mechanical devices and like all other mechanisms require servicing to keep them in prime condition. Some model engineers and amateur mechanics are inclined to treat their micrometers with so much respect that they are loth to take them apart! Fortunately, a new micrometer will give service for a long time before any attention is needed but sooner or later it will become advisable to take it apart for cleaning. Workshops are by nature dirty places and dust and dirt will eventually find its way into the micrometer. One indication that cleaning is required is when the thimble begins to get a little stiff to turn. This can be due to the original oil on the screw becoming sticky or the screw getting dirty – or both. There is nothing mystical or magical about the innards of a micrometer, they can be dismantled, cleaned, re-assembled and re-adjusted in just a few minutes time without the need for special tools or complicated incantations. In fact all that is needed is the spanner provided with every new micrometer and perhaps a screwdriver. Fig. 23 shows one of the author's micrometers dismantled. This type is now

out of production but such a vast number of these were made over a period of many years that they must still outnumber all of the other types put together. However, the basic components of the new range are still the same although Moore & Wrights have re-designed and simplified the spindle locking arrangement on all their micrometers.

To dismantle, start by screwing the thimble to open the anvil, but keep on rotating the thimble until the screw disengages the nut, which will be about fifteen or so turns after the last marking on the sleeve has been passed. The spindle should now pull out easily from the frame. Next, with the special spanner provided, unscrew and remove the ratchet assembly. The thimble can now be removed from the spindle. This could be quite tight but only friction is holding it in place. If it cannot be removed by finger pressure alone then carefully grip the spindle in the bench vice using soft jaws or, preferably, two pieces of wood, one on each side of the spindle. Very little pressure will now be required and twisting the thimble will then remove it easily from the spindle. Now remove the locking ring from the frame: this can only move one way owing to its being located in the frame by a small key. If you look on the 'back' side of the frame you will see the

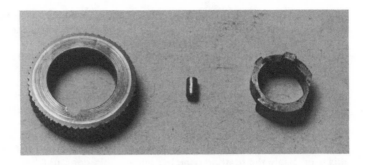

keyway by the side of the knurled ring, and keeping it in this position with the keyway facing you, a gentle pressure with the finger pushing the ring towards you will remove the locking ring assembly from the frame. This assembly consists of three pieces, the ring itself, the centre sleeve – a peculiar shaped piece – and a small pin. All the parts of the micrometer can now be washed to clean them and then wiped dry. The author finds petrol ideal for the cleaning fluid but if this is used all the usual fire precautions must be taken and, of course, make sure that the workshop is adequately ventilated. Paraffin is safer to use and will also give a satisfactory result.

The parts can now be re-assembled. Start with the locking ring assembly; as can be seen, this is really a roller ratchet. Place the ring on a flat surface – it does not matter which way up – and lifting the inner sleeve by the little projecting key or nib, drop it into place inside the ring. Not only has this sleeve got a key, it is also split to allow it to close onto the spindle and thus give the locking pressure. It also has a flat on it, which is not the location for the pin but is to help reduce the rigidity of the sleeve and allow it to close onto the spindle without undue pressure. The sleeve must be placed inside the ring in such a manner that the feature that looks like a ratchet tooth is positioned at the edge of the slot, allowing room for the pin to be placed in the slot. It is an advantage to have a small pair of tweezers to drop the pin into position. Should you have the misfortune to drop the pin on the floor and lose it, no great loss has been suffered as the pin is merely a short piece of 1/16in. dia. silver steel.

The photograph, fig. 24, shows the three items (greatly enlarged) that make up the locking ring assembly. The parts assembled are shown in the photograph, fig. 23. This assembly can now be put back into position in the frame, making sure that the small key enters into the keyway. Now, examine the spindle; a close look at the screw will show that the thread is truncated, which means that the curved top of the thread has been removed and that the thread form is flat across the top. This does not mean that the thread is weaker than the normal form of thread since only the sides or flanks of threads engage with each other and the curved top, being out of engagement, performs no useful function. In fact the author always truncates all threads when screwcutting as a matter of form. In this case the truncated thread is a distinct advantage as it provides pockets for lubricating oil and is one reason why, once cleaned and oiled, the micrometer will give a long period of service before needing further attention.

If the micrometer has been badly neglected and the thread has become rusty, apply a little "Brasso" and run the thread up and down the nut a few times until stiffness due to the rust has been removed. This may sound drastic but it is not. In fact the author has been recently informed by a production engineer at a micrometer manufacturing company that this is precisely the method used to rectify a 'rusty' screw when an instrument is returned to the factory for a manufacturer's service. The threads are hardened and the person screwing the thread in and out will get tired long before any measurable wear on the threads has taken place. All traces of the Brasso should, of course, be removed by washing in a solvent such as paraffin before the micrometer is re-assembled.

Referring back to the frame assembly it will be noticed that the outside of the nut is also threaded and split. A small ring nut is screwed onto this thread, refer to fig.23, this is a thread-adjusting nut and screwing this nut further onto the thread has the effect of closing-in the main or micrometer nut; moving it backwards will, of course, allow the main nut to open. It is therefore possible to compensate for wear in the micrometer screw and nut. When adjusted correctly the spindle should move freely through the main nut but without shake or backlash. The adjusting nut will have a hole or dimple in it so that it can be turned by the 'C' spanner provided. There is also a small ring nut on the end of the spindle – also shown in fig. 23. This determines the axial position of the thimble. If, when the micrometer is assembled and set at zero, the edge of the thimble does not coincide with the engraved line on the sleeve, then it can be adjusted by moving this nut. Screwing the nut further onto the spindle wil move the thimble nearer to the frame. Backing the nut off will have the effect of moving the thimble away from the frame.

The thimble can now be replaced onto the screw; push the thimble down until the bottom face butts up to the nut on the screw and replace the unit back into the micrometer frame. Put a drop of light oil onto the screw before the final assembly. This does not have to be special oil, the light machine oil normally used on the lathe mandrel will be satisfactory. When the anvil and spindle meet, the zero mark on the thimble should be on – or nearly on – the long datum or fiducial line on the sleeve. If it is not then rotate the thimble until it is so. The ratchet can now be screwed in. It will be noticed that the screw on the ratchet has a conical end and this cone fits into an internal cone in the spindle end. Since the spindle end is split, tightening up the ratchet also expands the spindle into the thimble and locks the two components together. Now close the micrometer by means of the ratchet – in all probability the zero setting on the thimble will be slightly out of register with the datum on the sleeve. If this is so then the sleeve needs rotating to get the two zero marks to correspond. The sleeve is a tight fit on the barrel but it is capable of being moved. It will be noticed that the sleeve has a small hole in it on the 'back' side. The 'C' spanner provided will engage into this hole and provide a means of rotating the sleeve to obtain the correct position. The micrometer is now ready again to give another long spell of good and faithful service.

The spindle locking feature now fitted in the current range of micrometers produced by Moore & Wright is a simpler design than that fitted on the earlier models. Instead of a clamp ring encircling the spindle, the spindle is merely pushed over to one side of its bore by a brass pinch screw. Purists of design could argue that this modern production method is an inferior and retrogade step, and maybe from their point of view it is; however, it does work very effectively and must be much easier and cheaper to produce, and any acceptable feature that can reduce the cost to the home workshop user is certainly a feature worthy of careful consideration. The photograph, fig. 25, shows this locking device dismantled and as can be seen, it is possible to take it apart for periodic cleaning without removing any other feature of the micrometer. To do this, first set the lever in the unlocked position, thus removing any load that would otherwise be acting on the locking screw, then, with a small sharp screwdriver, remove the small slot-headed screw which is only holding the small lever in position. Next, lift the lever off the brass clamp screw and it will be immediately apparent that this screw has a serrated or splined head and that the underside of the lever is provided with a mating serrated hole. Once the lever has been removed the locking screw, which will not be tight, can be easily removed by the normal unscrewing action – no spanner will be required. The only other part to be removed is the curved washer that fits between the head of the clamping screw and the micrometer body.

After cleaning the parts it takes only a minute or so to re-assemble. First place the curved washer in the spotfacing provided. Although this washer can be positioned in two different ways, only one way is correct – the curved face must be uppermost. Next replace the clamping screw and screw down until the end of the screw meets the micrometer spindle. The

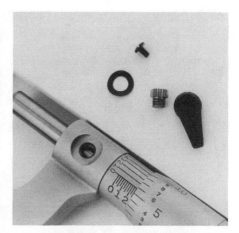

Fig.25 This shows a dismantled alternative spindle-locking device – the small brass screw makes contact with the spindle and so provides the locking force. This photograph also shows the vernier scale that is provided on some micrometers.

underside of the clampscrew head should also be in contact with the curved washer; this places a slight pre-load on the clampscrew and prevents the lever from 'flapping about' when the device is not locking the spindle. Next place the lever over the serration and position so that the spindle is effectively clamped before the limit of lever travel is reached. You may not get the lever on the correct serration first time but it will be obvious at once whether to move one serration to the right or left to obtain the desired position. Finally, replace and tighten the small slot-headed screw.

Special micrometers are produced for measuring inside holes, and these are naturally termed 'inside micrometers'. As can be seen by looking at fig. 26, these are really a measuring head similar to that of an ordinary micrometer but generally with a smaller movement. The usual amount of movement is a half-inch or 10mm, but heads of a quarter-inch or

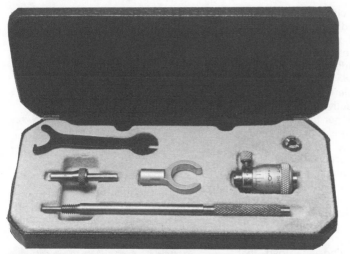

Fig.26 An inside micrometer set in its case. This is one of the smaller sets available and has a range of one to two inches. The micrometer head has a movement of only .250 inches and the range is increased by removable anvils and a distance collar. The distance collar which is .250" long is shown in the top right hand corner of the box. The permutations of assembly are (1)the head as shown giving a range of 1" to $1\frac{1}{4}$"; (2) as above but with the distance collar fitted — $1\frac{1}{4}$" to $1\frac{1}{2}$"; (3) the standard anvil changed for the extended one — $1\frac{1}{2}$" to $1\frac{3}{4}$"; (4) as above but with the distance collar fitted — $1\frac{3}{4}$" to 2".

Fig.27a. Placing the inside micrometer into a bore prior to measuring. The extended handle is only used on the small instrument when the bore is not large enough to accommodate the operator's finger.

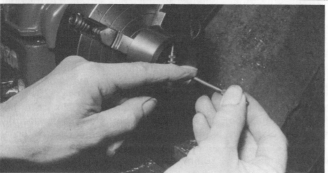

Fig.27b. Sizing the bore. One anvil of the micrometer is kept in firm contact with the bore of the workpiece by applying pressure with the first finger, the micrometer is then pivoted above this point, the rocking action being supplied via the extension handle. The whole action is basically similar to the one used with inside calipers.

34

5mm are produced. Even with the smaller heads the smallest hole that will allow the micrometer to enter is one-inch or 25mm diameter. Extension rods are provided which increase the range and allow quite large bores to be gauged using the one micrometer head. Their use is not limited to holes or bores, however, as they can also be used for measuring between faces or height above a datum, such as from a surface table to a feature on a component resting on the surface table. They are certainly more difficult to use than the normal outside type of micrometer and practice will be needed before they can be used with confidence.

One point particularly to watch out for when using an inside micrometer – or any of the larger micrometers – is thermal expansion. Obviously the larger sizes are more susceptible to thermal expansion than the smaller ones. A few degrees difference in temperature between the micrometer and the workpiece will not make much noticeable difference when measuring a distance of one inch but if the distance being gauged is 10 inches or so then the effects of temperature differences may have to be considered. As the body temperature of the operator is usually well above the workshop temperature, the reading should be taken quickly before the heat from the hands passes into the micrometer. Because the majority of holes produced in the model engineer's or amateur workshop will be under, rather than over, one-inch diameter an inside micrometer would have only limited use and could be considered as a luxury item.

Another type of micrometer which has limited use is the micrometer depth gauge. This is a device for measuring the depth of holes, or the size of steps or shoulders. The gauge consists of a flat surface from which protrudes an adjustable probe. This probe is in fact an extension to the normal micrometer spindle head. It follows that the spindle face must be coincident with the head or datum face when the thimble is in the screwed-out position, and gives its maximum reading

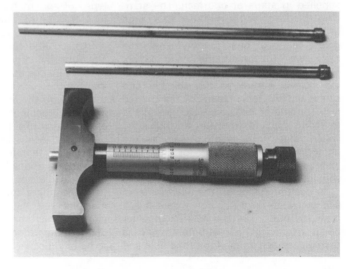

Fig.28 Depth micrometer. The spindle fitted will provide a range of 0-1-inch; two further rods are shown, one giving a range of 1"-2" and the other increasing the range to 2"-3".

with the thimble "screwed-in". This reversal from the normal movement means that the graduations on both sleeve and thimble are reversed. The sleeve engravings are read from right to left and the value of the spindle markings rises as the thimble is "screwed-in". It is obvious that the reversal is necessary and, in fact, when in use, the operator is usually oblivious of the fact that the scales are reversed!

This type of micrometer must be used with care as it is very easy to obtain an incorrect reading. When the probe makes contact with the bottom face of the hole being measured, it is very easy to screw the thimble too far and so lift the micrometer head off the datum face. Once again it is a case of developing the correct feel. Fig.28 shows an example of the depth micrometer. The knurled nut on the end of the thimble is not a ratchet, it is in fact the nut which captures the spindle or probe. In order to increase the range of the depth micrometer, extension spindles can be fitted, each of these spindles being supplied in steps of one inch. The standard spindle gives the micrometer a range of zero to one-inch, the next spindle will give a range of one- to two-inches, the next, two- to three-inches, and so on. These replaceable spindles pass through the hollow centre of the thimble and screw and are held in place by the knurled nut. The end of each extension spindle is threaded and fitted with an adjusting collar, these are clearly seen in the photograph, thus allowing for small adjustments in effective spindle lengths should these become necessary.

In use the spindle of the micrometer is screwed back to a position where it will clear the bottom of the hole or shoulder being gauged. The instrument head is then placed across the top of the hole and

firmly held there whilst the spindle is screwed down until the end-face of the spindle just touches the work. It is only possible to use a micrometer depth gauge where a satisfactory seating for its datum face can be found, and the bottom of the hole or slot being measured must be parallel to this seating.

Rule type depth gauges are also available, these being much simpler and cheaper than the micrometer type. These consist of a very narrow rule to which a sliding head is clamped; the rule is usually calibrated with imperial scale on one side and metric on the reverse. To change from one to the other is a simple matter, just slide the rule out of its guiding slot, turn it over and replace it.

There are many special types of micrometers manufactured and it is the same with micrometers as with rules, different trades require different features on their tools to accommodate their special needs. There are micrometers made with large flanged anvils and these are used for measuring paper and other types of soft material where a large surface area on the anvil is required to prevent the anvil from sinking into the workpiece and so giving a false reading. The tube industry requires a micrometer to measure the thickness of tube walls but the standard anvil is of little use here as the anvil on the inside of the tube would only be touching the workpiece on the outer edges. To overcome this, special ball-ended anvils are made; this type of micrometer therefore has the spindle-end flat and the anvil in the frame hemispherical in shape.

If the sheet metal worker wishes to measure the thickness of a sheet, the standard micrometer is of little use as the depth of the frame will only allow readings to be taken close to the edge of the sheet.

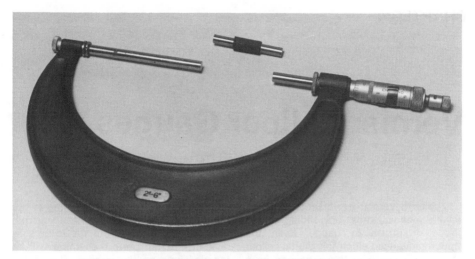

Fig.29 The 'outside' micrometer usually has a range of one-inch, this means that quite a number of instruments may be needed to cover the range up to, say, 6-inches. The micrometer shown has replaceable anvils and so will cover the complete range from 2" to 6". A standard is provided for each interchangeable anvil so that the accuracy may be checked. Tha main objection the author has found to this system is that when set for the smaller sizes the whole instrument is large and cumbersome.

To overcome this problem the sheet metal micrometer has a very deep frame with a working depth of about six inches. In order to keep rigidity, a frame of this size has to have a deep section and this makes this type of micrometer very cumbersome, but since it is only intended for measuring sheets, this is of no consequence. The opposite of this micrometer is the one used in the manufacture of milling cutters. In order to permit insertion into the relatively small bore so that the thickness of the cutter boss can be measured, the micrometer frame must be shallow. The screw-thread industry requires micrometers with pointed anvils so that measurements can be taken over a screw; this type is extra special as allowance must be made for errors due to the helix angle of the screw.

There are many more types of micrometers but all of these special tools are of little use to the model engineer or home mechanic. A standard zero to one-inch and, possibly, a one-inch to two-inch micrometer will be adequate to perform all, or nearly all, the gauging work he will be called upon to undertake.

CHAPTER 4

Vernier Caliper Gauges

The term 'vernier' in workshop parlance usually means almost any sliding caliper gauge or protractor gauge. Even the modern advanced electronic digital caliper is still referred to in the workshop as a 'vernier' although it does not carry any vernier scale at all. In actual fact, a vernier is only a special type of scale which allows far more accurate readings to be obtained than could otherwise be achieved from the ordinary scale used on rules or protractors. The quickest way to understand the principle of the vernier scale is to examine the scale applied to a micrometer as this is probably the simplest and most familiar of all vernier scales. As discussed in the last chapter, readings to three decimal places can be obtained from the normal micrometer but the marks on the thimble will not always coincide with the datum line on the thimble. If it were possible to divide the .001 divisions on the thimble into 10 parts then, assuming we could actually see those lines, readings of one-tenth of a thou could be obtained. It is, of course, not practical to split one of the thimble divisions into 10 parts and so some other means must be found if readings of four places of decimals are required. This is where we use the vernier scale. Any vernier scale consists of a number of divisions corresponding to the fraction of the main division required; thus, if the main divisions are to be subdivided into ten parts then there will be ten divisions on the vernier. This is the case with the micrometer when we have to divide the .001 thimble divisions into ten parts to obtain readings of .0001 increments. Therefore this vernier scale will have to be provided with ten divisions. The vernier scale is made to a length just one division less than the main scale, which means that the full length of the 10 vernier divisions is only as long as 9 divisions of the main or thimble scale on the micrometer. This can be quickly checked. If you have a micrometer fitted with a vernier scale, set the thimble in such a position that the zero line corresponds with the sleeve datum. It will be seen that the tenth division on the vernier scale /marked zero) will be coincident with the ninth mark on the thimble scale. As a result of this each vernier division is equivalent to nine-tenths of the main division, or put another way, each vernier scale is one-tenth short of a thimble division. The micrometer shown in close-up in fig.25 is fitted with a vernier scale and this photograph clearly shows that the divisions of the vernier are smaller than the thimble divisions. It follows therefore that two vernier divisions are two-tenths short, three vernier divisions are three-tenths short and so on. The vernier scale is placed next to the main scale.

In the case of the micrometer the vernier scale is placed on the sleeve with the vernier lines running the full length of the sleeve and, of course, parallel to the main fiducial line. As discussed above, if the zero mark on the thimble is placed in line with this fiducial line then it will be seen that the tenth, or last, vernier scale line will be coincident to the ninth thimble line, and that no other two lines in the vernier scale will match any thimble lines. But if, say, the scales are placed so that the seventh vernier line coincides with a line on the thimble then seven divisions on the vernier will be shorter than seven divisions on the thimble by seven-tenths of one of the thimble divisions. In the case of an imperial micrometer this will represent a

spindle movement equal to .0007 inches. It is not necessary to have all this in mind when taking a reading from the vernier scale. Just observe the number on the vernier scale which coincides with a main scale graduation and, in the case of the micrometer, this represents the fourth figure in a decimal reading. Fig.30 shows diagrammatically a micrometer reading using the vernier scale. An interesting point is the position of the vernier scale: it need not be based about the thimble datum line, it could be moved further round the sleeve providing that it registers zero when the datum line coincides with a thimble graduation.

Vernier scales can also be fitted to metric micrometers and this enables the reading to be obtained in increments of .002mm. Whether the vernier micrometer is an advantage to the model engineer is open to question. It is one thing to have the facility of obtaining a reading to these

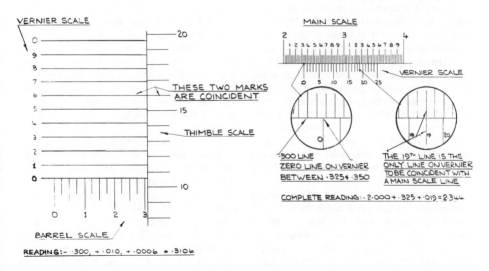

Fig.30 Diagrammatic view of a vernier scale fitted to a micrometer.

Fig.31 Diagrammatic view showing a reading on a vernier caliper gauge.

39

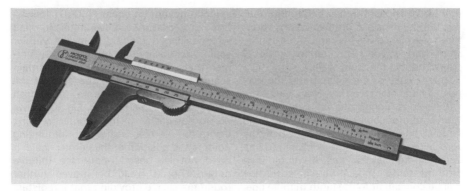

Fig.32 This shows a 'standard' six-inch vernier caliper gauge. The sliding jaw is moved by pressing the serrated lever by means of the thumb and then pushing in the direction required. On more sophisticated gauges fine adjustment is made easier by means of a screw and nut assembly which is attached to the sliding jaw.

extraordinarily fine limits but whether the reading obtained is in actual fact the size of the workpiece is another matter.

Although the micrometer is a very useful tool, it has disadvantages and the main one is that it possesses a limited range because for practical reasons each instrument is limited to one inch of movement. It is therefore necessary to have several instruments in order to cover most requirements. It is true that micrometers with removable anvils are produced and one such instrument will cover all sizes from two inches to six inches. The frame, of course, has to be large enough to cover the six inch size so this makes the micrometer somewhat cumbersome, particularly if fitted with the long anvil needed to obtain the two- to three-inch range. Fig.29 shows a micrometer of this type.

This is where the vernier caliper gauge has an advantage, since it can be made to any length within reason – the six-inch is very popular – and it will measure accurately to anywhere within its range. With the imperial vernier the main or basic rule scale is divided into tenths of an inch. These tenths are further divided into four

equal parts and these parts (subdivisions) are therefore equal to .025 inches. This means that the main scale will give a direct reading in units of .025. Spacings of .025in. can be easily distinguished by a person with normal eyesight, however, most vernier users keep a magnifying glass close at hand! The vernier scale is applied in a similar way as it is in the micrometer to obtain the number of thousandths to be added to get a complete reading, the main difference being that the vernier scale has twenty-five divisions and they are equal to twenty-four on the main scale. The principle, however, is exactly the same as was described for the micrometer.

To obtain a reading add the number of inches, tenths of inches and 25-thousandths together, and then add the number of thousandths indicated by the vernier graduation which coincides with a rule scale graduation. Fig.31 shows diagrammatically a reading of 2.344in.; however, in the diagram the vernier scale has been made "twice-size", or, instead of using a space of twenty-four .025 divisions, it has used a space of twenty-four .050 divisions. This, in fact, is often done

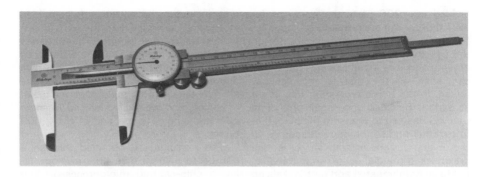

Fig.33 On the gauge shown here the vernier scale has been replaced by a dial gauge which is much easier to read but, as the dial is mechanically driven, there is the possibility that errors could arise.

on the actual gauge as it makes the reading of the scale much easier; the vernier shown in photograph fig.32 employs a scale of this type. There are some vernier gauges where the main scale is divided into .050 divisions rather than .025 and these then use a vernier scale of 50 divisions based on a length of 49 divisions on the main scale.

Once the actual principle of the vernier scale has been understood, it will be realised that it is capable of being used in a variety of ways. Since the gauge is only using one edge of what is really a rule, the remaining edge is usually used for metric graduations, therefore most vernier gauges have both imperial and metric scales. Of the many verniers the author has come into contact with, it has always been the practice to have the upper scale for the metric graduations and the lower one for the imperial.

The correct reading of a vernier caliper gauge depends to a great extent on the good eyesight of the operator, far more so than with the micrometer. As will have been seen, reading a micrometer to one-tenth of a thousandth of an inch is easier on the eye than obtaining a reading of one-thou on a vernier caliper.

DIAL CALIPER GAUGE

The dial caliper gauge has been introduced in an attempt to ease the reading problem. With this instrument the vernier scale has been removed and replaced with a dial gauge. The dial gauge is driven by means of a rack and pinion. The rack, which must be of great precision, is placed in a groove usually down the centre of the 'rule' and between the two scales. Often a cover is provided to give protection to the rack, but even so this protection is lost when the gauge jaws are opened so care must be taken not to allow dirt or swarf to enter into the rack, otherwise damage could occur. The author has had a gauge of this type now for a good many years and no problems have been experienced with the rack mechanism.

The main scale on this type of gauge is usually divided into tenths of an inch only. This makes it very easy to read. The next two decimal places are obtained from the dial which usually has a range of .200 inches. This means that to give a reading in thousandths over a range of .100 inches, the dial scale is split into two halves, each half reading zero to 100. The dials are $1\frac{1}{4}$in. to $1\frac{1}{2}$in. diameter and as the dial is divided into 200 parts the markings for each thousandth are rather close together, but even so they are certainly easier on the eye than the vernier scale. It can be argued, and it is a valid point, that errors can arise as the dial is mechanically driven. In the home workshop this is not so serious because once again the same tool will be used to measure the parts that fit together and so the gauge becomes, in the main, a comparator. There is one drawback in the dial caliper in that it does not have both imperial and metric dials on the one tool, they are either all imperial or all metric. Fig.33 shows a dial caliper gauge.

ELECTRONIC DIGITAL CALIPER

Recent developments in the rapidly growing field of electronics have enabled a new type of gauge to be developed, known as the electronic digital caliper, fig.34. This is certainly an important advance and eliminates the reading of scales completely, the size measured being clearly presented in large numbers on a high contrast L.C.D. display. The whole measuring unit, including the batteries, is contained in a space no larger than the normal vernier scale or dial gauge. The batteries used are silver oxide and it is claimed by the manufacturers that one pair will give about 2,000 hours continuous use. They are very small, about the size of one tablet of aspirin, and are easily replaced when an operator comes to the end of the 2,000 hours!

The readings are obtained through a non-contact linear measuring system using a chip-centred microprocessor. The display can be switched to read either imperial or metric scales, the resolution usually being .0005in. on the imperial and .01mm on the metric display. The display is also provided with a zero reset feature. This can be used anywhere on the scale: a press of a small button and the display will read zero. Any movement that subsequently takes place will be registered on the scale and it will also show whether it is in a plus or minus direction thus allowing deviations from a set standard to be directly determined. This reset device also provides automatic compensation for any

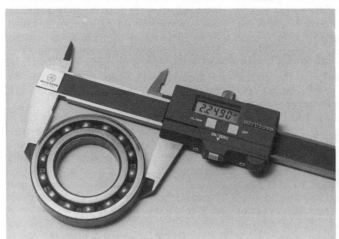

Fig.34 An electronic digital caliper gauge. These are the simplest of all to read as the display is clear and large. Since the readings are obtained from a 'non-contact' system they should be free from errors due to mechanical wear but it must not be forgotten that when electronic equipment does go wrong it is usually on a grand scale!

wear that could take place over a period of time, thus eliminating the need for recalibration. After using the reset button in mid-scale, if the caliper jaws are brought back together again and the button re-pressed the display will return to zero and the gauge is immediately ready for normal use again.

In use all types of caliper gauges are capable of undertaking the same type of work. The obvious, and main purpose, is to measure between the two jaws for determining length. It may be the length of a piece of material or bar, or it may be the length of some feature such as a shoulder, either after or during machining. It is also possible to measure diameters between the jaws, although the range of diameter that can be measured in this way will depend on the length of the jaws, the maximum diameter being twice the length of the jaws. Diameters greater than this can be obtained by gauging over the end of the workpiece. To assist in getting into awkward places such as undercuts, not only are the jaws tapered but they are usually thinned down to almost a knife edge. Inside measurements, not only of diameters but of grooves, slots or keyways, are obtained by using the inside jaws. These are much smaller than the main jaws and are situated on the op-

posite side to the main jaw but they are made so that they close at the same time, thus allowing the one scale to apply to both sets of jaws. The jaws are knife-edged for the complete length, thus minimising any error when used to measure inside diameters. They are not intended for small holes but give satisfactory results on holes above half-an-inch or so.

All the caliper gauges described in these notes are fitted with depth gauges. This allows the depth of holes or shoulders to be obtained and could be used as an alternative to a depth micrometer or ordinary depth gauge. The depth gauge is at the opposite end to the jaws and consists of a strip of material secured to the sliding body of the gauge and usually running in a groove down the centre of the rule portion. When the jaws are closed together the length of the strip is such that it is coincident with the square end of the gauge. Since it moves in unison with the moving jaw it follows that the projection over the end face of the gauge is exactly the same as the jaw opening so the gauge reading applies both to the jaws and the depth gauge. In the case of the dial caliper gauge, the depth gauge often forms the protective covers for the rack, which is why the rack at the

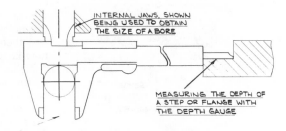

INTERNAL JAWS, SHOWN BEING USED TO OBTAIN THE SIZE OF A BORE

MEASURING THE DEPTH OF A STEP OR FLANGE WITH THE DEPTH GAUGE

Fig.35 Showing three common uses of the vernier caliper gauge. The one reading shown on the scale applies to all three applications.

EXTERNAL JAWS BEING USED TO DETERMINE THE DIAMETER OF A SHAFT jaw end of the gauge becomes uncovered as the jaws are opened. The diagram, fig.35, illustrates the three basic types of measurement that can be carried out with a normal vernier caliper gauge and shows how the one reading applies to all three functions.

There are occasions when a size of a feature is required and it cannot be obtained by a simple direct measurement. The case shown in fig.36 is a typical example. Here it is required to know the thickness of the material between the bottom of the hole and the outer edge or end face of the component. Clearly this cannot be ascertained by simple direct measurement. The required thickness has to be obtained by first measuring other features and then by simple calculation. The vernier type caliper gauge is ideally suited for this type of application. First measure the total thickness of the component, size 'A' on fig.36, using the normal outside jaws. It is advisable to write this down otherwise the chances are that it will be forgotten! Then, using the depth gauge of the caliper, obtain the depth of the hole. It is important to make sure that the end face of the gauge is in contact with the

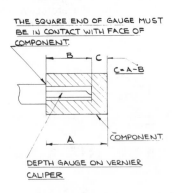

THE SQUARE END OF GAUGE MUST BE IN CONTACT WITH FACE OF COMPONENT.

DEPTH GAUGE ON VERNIER CALIPER

Fig.36 Determining the thickness of an end wall.

face of the component and also square with it otherwise an incorrect reading will be obtained. The size required is now obtained by subtracting the second reading from the first.

The electronic caliper gauge fitted with a digital readout simplifies this procedure by performing the calculation for you and giving the size required directly on the display. The procedure is basically as before but this time use the depth gauge first; however, do not note the reading, simply press the reset button − the display will then register zero. Then, using the outside jaws, measure the outside or 'A' dimension in fig.36. Now, when the jaws are opened to a size equal to the depth of the hole, the display will show zero and will only then begin to rise. It therefore follows that when the jaws have reached the 'A' dimension the display will in fact be registering the size required, or the 'C' dimension. The instrument has done the calculation for you!

Another example where direct measurement is not practical is in finding the centre distance between two holes. It is not feasible to measure from a centre line of a hole because the centre line is only a line in space and is not a tangible object; the only thing that can be used as a measuring datum is the edge of the hole itself. Reference to fig.37 shows the method used. First, with the inside jaws of the vernier, measure the diameters of both the holes, add these two sizes together and then divide by two, thus if the first hole is 1.000in. dia. and the second hole 1.250in. dia., we will have 1.000 + 1.250 which is 2.250, divided by two this becomes 1.125. If the distances between the two outer edges of the holes is 6 inches, then the centre distance is 6 − 1.125 which is 4.875in. In theory it is possible to measure the distance between

44

the two inner edges of the holes and add half the hole sizes, but do not do this. The outside jaws of the vernier are feathered for their entire length; the inside jaws, if they are chamfered, will only be thinned down for a small distance, and if the full jaw thickness is used to measure between the two holes an incorrect reading will certainly be obtained. Should the two holes both be the same size then the process is simplified, merely subtract the hole size from the distance 'D' in fig.37. Owners of an electronic gauge will, of course, realise that it is possible to let the gauge do the calculation for you!

Caliper gauges are not as simple to use as a micrometer but with a little practice the skills required to achieve satisfactory results can be quickly acquired. As with all other measuring tools discussed, the main thing to remember and aim for is the correct sense of touch. It is not so easy to 'clamp' or overtighten the workpiece between the jaws of a caliper gauge as the jaws are not moved by means of a screw, as is the spindle of a micrometer, but by sliding the measuring head along the body of the gauge by means of the thumb of the right hand. The

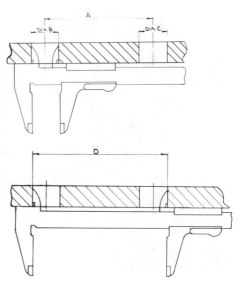

HOLE CENTRE DISTANCE $A = $ DISTANCE $D - \dfrac{(\text{DIA.B} + \text{DIA.C})}{2}$

Fig.37 Determining the centre distance of two holes using a vernier caliper gauge.

amount of force that can be applied by this method is limited and so the tendency to overtighten the gauge is largely eliminated. In the case of the dial caliper

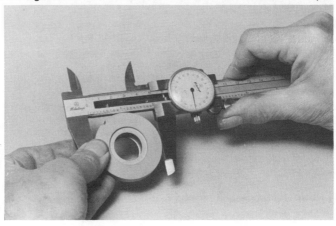

Fig.38 Showing how to hold the vernier gauge when sizing a hand-held workpiece. The gauge is controlled entirely by the right hand, the left hand supplies a steady support for the gauge and also holds the workpiece in the correct attitude. Measuring diameters in this way is limited not by the length of the instrument but by the depth of the jaws.

Fig. 39 Measuring the bore of a component that has not yet been removed from the lathe. The right hand is controlling the gauge but the left hand is providing a platform on which to rest the jaws. If the outer face of the component is square to the bore, the entire length of the outside jaws can be inserted into the bore so that the face of the gauge is touching the face of the workpiece. This will ensure that the gauge is square to the workpiece.

the jaw is moved by means of a small knurled wheel which only has friction contact with the slide and so which basically functions in a similar way to the ratchet of a micrometer.

The caliper gauge is basically a right-handed tool, although two hands are often used in the act of measuring, the left hand being used mainly as a steady for the fixed jaw. This becomes more important as the

Fig.40 Sizing a diameter 'over the end'. This method can be used up to the limit of the gauge. The fixed jaw is held in the left hand which is also keeping the jaw in contact with the workpiece; the whole gauge is then pivoted about this point by moving the right hand up and down.

workpiece gets larger because best use will not be obtained if one end of the gauge is waving about and not under full control. The photographs, figs.38, 39 and 40 illustrate three different types of workpiece being measured and show how the gauge is held in each case. As mentioned above the caliper gauge is very much a right-handed tool and if the operator is left-handed problems will arise because if the tool is held in the normal manner but in the left hand, it will be impossible to read the scale as the whole tool will be upside-down and the workpiece will have to be removed and the gauge turned over for the reading to be obtained. This can of course increase the risk of an incorrect reading. The author has tried using a vernier in the left hand and achieved the best results by holding the tool face upwards but with the jaws pointing away from him, the moving jaw being operated by means of the first finger of the left hand. The scales are, of course, upside-down but it is possible to read them.

CHAPTER 5

Dial Gauges

Dial gauges are instruments that are capable of sensing or detecting small movements or size variations in a workpiece and then magnifying these movements in such a way that they can be registered on a dial. This dial is reminiscent of a clock face, in fact the dial gauge is often referred to in the workshop as the "clock". There are a great many types of instruments used in engineering fitted with dials, most of them used in industrial inspection departments. However, from our point of view the dial gauge is an instrument with a face over which sweeps a finger or pointer. This pointer is moved by a small button or contact point via a train of gears. The gear train 'magnifies' the movement imparted to the button by the workpiece.

The dial can be calibrated in a number of ways, some dials having a range of .100in. per revolution and the scales of these dials are usually calibrated into 100 divisions which means that every division represents .001in. movement on the operating button. The scale may be from 0 to 100, or it may be from 0 to 50 and back again to zero. Other gauges have much smaller full scale deflection which may be only .010. These sensitive gauges may be calibrated in increments of one-

tenth of a thousandth-of-an-inch and are intended in the main for high class inspection work. They are not ideally suited for model work as they are much too sensitive. In the amateur's workshop the author has found that a dial registering 0-25-0 gives complete satisfaction for most cases where the use of a dial gauge is required. The range of button, or stylus, movement can also vary considerably, some gauges accommodating a total movement of half-an-inch or so whilst the range on the very sensitive gauges may be as small as .010. Again, this latter type has very little use for model engineering needs.

Dial gauges can be divided into two further types, the plunger type gauge and the lever type dial indicator. The plunger type is the simplest of the designs, with the operating button screwed directly into the bottom of the plunger. This plunger then passes through the body of the gauge guided by two bearings, one on each side of the circular body or case, and between the two bearings a fine rack is cut into the plunger. A gear engages with this rack, this gear being the first in a train which increases the angular movement with the final gear being the one that drives the pointer. The plunger may also be mounted in the back of the case, and this type is called the 'back plunger' or 'perpendicular' gauge, and this places the dial at right-angles to the plunger rather than in line with it. The author has used both types of plunger dial gauge and has not found that one possesses any general advantage over the other. When used on small machines some people may prefer to be over the top and looking down at the dial rather than looking horizontally at it and if this is so then the back plunger gauge is the one to use, it is just a matter of personal preference.

The lever type of gauge is more complicated, the pointer or finger being fitted on the end of a coarse spiral worm and this worm is driven round by a system of levers which are operated by the button or stylus. When using the plunger type of gauge the body of the gauge will be directly over the plunger with the dial being in either the vertical or horizontal position depending on the style of gauge being used. This means that for direct readings the dial will be immediately over

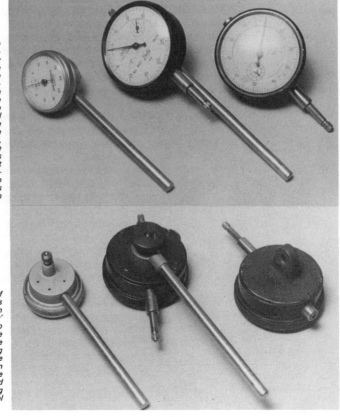

Fig.41a Showing three different types of dial calibrations, and there are many more! The small gauge on the left reads 0-25-0, the centre one also has the same deflection reading and tha one on the right has a full scale deflection of .100". The two larger gauges both have small secondary dials that count the number of revolutions the sweep pointer has made and, as can be seen, on one gaugethe small finger moves in a clockwise direction whilst the other one moves anticlockwise. This is of no significance but does emphasise just how dials can vary.

Fig.41b. The reverse side of the same three gauges. This shows that the small one is an example of a 'back plunger' gauge whilst on the other two the gauges are situated on the side of the casings. On the small gauge the mounting arm is rigidly fixed; on the centre example the arrm can be rotated but in one plane only, whilst the right hand gauge is provided with a lug for fastening on to a universal clamp.

the point of contact between the button and the workpiece and so space must be available over the point of contact to allow the gauge to be used. Naturally, this imposes limitations on its use and if the inside of a bore is to be the setting datum then the bore must be large enough to allow entry of the complete gauge. It cannot therefore be used directly in small holes or other restricted areas although there is a way of overcoming this problem – refer to fig.45. On the lever type of gauge, the stylus or button, being on the end of an operating lever, can penetrate into small holes or areas, the rest of the gauge being well out of the way.

The majority of all dial gauges are provided with movable calibrated dials secured to knurled bezels. This provides the facility of being able to rotate the dial to any desired angular positon, thus ensuring that the pointer can always be

aligned at zero. This is an advantage particularly if the dial is calibrated from zero up to half-scale deflection and then down to zero again as there is then a plus and minus reading available about the zero setting. It is then possible, when checking a number of similar pieces, to set the gauge to read zero at the correct dimension required. The reading then obtained when the gauge is applied to the workpiece will not only register the size of any error but also whether the workpiece is larger or smaller than the required nominal size.

In order to apply a dial gauge to a workpiece the gauge must be held in some way and the method of holding will depend to a large extent on the type and location of the workpiece. One method is the use of the base or stand. This consists of a vertical steel column – usually $\frac{1}{2}$in. diameter but this size may vary – secured to a heavy base. On commercial stands this base may be produced in cast-iron but if the stand is home made and cast-iron is not available then steel may be used. The base must be heavy compared to the rest of the stand because it is vitally important that the dial gauge is rigidly and securely held whilst readings are being taken. As the base will, in the majority of cases, be in contact with a cast-iron surface-plate or a lathe cross-slide or some other magnetic material, then a base containing a suitable magnet is a distinct advantage. This type of base is not only heavy and rigid but also the strong magnet built into it can be switched either on or off by pressing a button built into the base. When in the off position the base can be moved easily

Fig.42 This illustration shows a back plunger gauge mounted on a stand with a magnetic base. This combination is very useful when seting workpieces in machine tools but does have limitations owing to it being desirable to keep the mounting arm in either a horizontal or vertical position (refer to fig.46).

over a metal surface but when the button is pressed and the magnet is switched on, the base and complete stand is very firmly and rigidly held. So strong are these magnetic bases that the stand can be mounted at any angle, and even upside-down, and still give the necessary support to the dial gauge.

The dial gauge itself will be provided with a mounting arm which will be either rigidly fixed to the outer case or pivoted and furnished with a clamp screw. In either case a fitting will be required to secure the dial mounting onto the stand. This fitting is usually called a universal clamp. It is bored to pass over and slide up and down the stand and is also bored to allow the dial mounting rod to pass through it; one thumbscrew will lock both clamp and dial fixing arm in any desired position. The operating height of the gauge can, therefore, be set by moving the clamp up or down the stand and the distance from the stand to the dial gauge can also be adjusted by moving the mounting arm through the clamp. The

photograph, fig.42, shows an example of this type of arrangement. When using the plunger type of gauge it is important that the plunger is at right-angles to the workpiece, otherwise the reading obtained on the dial will not be the same as the distance being gauged, fig.46.

In the amateur workshop, the principal use of a dial gauge will be in assisting the setting of workpieces in the lathe, milling or shaping machine. The stand just described can be used on all these machines but when used in the lathe an alternative method of mounting the dial may be required. When a dial gauge is being used to set up a workpiece in the lathe, the idea is to set a datum surface on the workpiece to run truly in relation to the tool to be used. It may therefore be an advantage to mount the dial gauge in the tool holder itself. Mounted in this fashion the gauge can be moved about the workpiece by means of the cross-slide and carriage and this can be very useful as not only can the workpiece be set to run truly, it can also be set square. If the workpiece

Fig.43 Setting a disc, or in this case a wheel, square with the lathe axis. The gauge is secured in the tool holder which gives the gauge a rigid mounting and also provides the facility of a controlled movement.

Fig.44 This shows the gauge stand combination depicted in fig.42 being used to set a workpiece parallel to a milling machine table. It is an ideal unit for this type of work.

is flat or disc-shaped, then the button of the gauge can be set first on the outer rim in order to set the disc to run truly, then the gauge can be moved so that the button makes contact with the face of the disc, at or near the largest diameter, and rotating the lathe by hand will then show at once whether the disc is set square or not. After setting square the dial gauge can be traversed over the face of the disc by means of the cross-slide feed screw. This will indicate whether or not the disc is flat as any movement of the pointer will show that the disc is slightly conical. If, after taking a facing cut across the disc, the last test is repeated, it will indicate whether the lathe is facing square!

A gauge mounted in the tool rest can also be used in setting up cylindrical workpieces or shafts both axially true and square. To do this use the gauge near to the chuck in order to get the workpiece to run truly at that point, then with the button of the dial gauge still in contact with the workpiece, move the gauge along the workpiece by means of the lathe

carriage handwheel until the end of the workpiece or the gauged diameter is reached, then rotate the lathe. If the workpiece is out of square with the lathe mandrel there will be a deflection shown on the dial. It must be remembered when using a dial gauge on a rotating component that the deflection shown on the dial is twice the actual eccentricity of the component and that the movement required to obtain true-running is, therefore, only a half of the error registered on the dial of the gauge.

When used in the milling or shaping machine, the main purpose of the gauge will be to set the upper face of the workpiece parallel to the machine table. It is most likely that in our small workshops the component will be held in one or two machine vices as shown in fig.44. Set the component in the vices first by 'eye', and if two vices are being used and they are a 'matched' pair it is surprising just how accurately the eye can judge! Use the dial gauge mounted on a stand and should the stand be fitted with a magnetic base

Fig.45 It is not possible to get a plunger type of gauge inside a small bore; however, by using the angled attachment shown fitted to the gauge it is possible to gain entry into quite small holes.

switch this to the 'off' position as it is necessary to be able to move the stand quickly from one place to another. Place the gauge so that the button is touching the workface at one end of the component then rotate the dial until the needle registers zero. Next, and without moving anything else, move the stand and gauge unit to the other end of the component and take a reading on the workface there. If the component is not parallel to the machine table the gauge will register the error and it will also show whether the error is in the 'plus' or 'minus' direction. When readings taken at both ends of the component correspond then subsequent readings taken at intermediate points along its length will indicate whether the workpiece is flat or bowed.

Tests for roundness can also be made with the dial gauge, in fact this may be the only way an amateur can test roundness. It must be appreciated that when the diameter of a cylinder is being measured by means of caliper or micrometer, it is not roundness that is being measured but a simple linear size from one point to another. Taking a number of similar readings at different points around the circumference does not indicate roundness

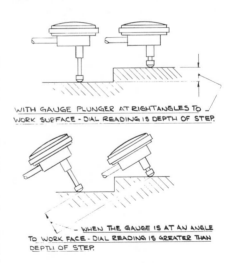

WITH GAUGE PLUNGER AT RIGHTANGLES TO WORK SURFACE - DIAL READING IS DEPTH OF STEP.

WHEN THE GAUGE IS AT AN ANGLE TO WORK FACE - DIAL READING IS GREATER THAN DEPTH OF STEP.

Fig.46 Showing the effect of applying a dial gauge at an angle to the workpiece.

53

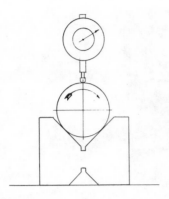

THE WORKPIECE IS ROTATED IN VEE BLOCK.
ERRORS IN ROUNDNESS WILL BE INDICATED
BY A NEEDLE DEFLECTION

Fig.47 Test for roundness.

either. Certain shapes appear to be round when measured in this way but in actual fact they may not be so. To test for roundness three points of contact are necessary and this can be achieved by placing the component on a vee-block and rotating it under a dial indicator as shown in fig.47. If the component is accurately centred at both ends then it may, of course, be freely rotated between these centres in the lathe for the tests to be made.

It will be realised from the above discussion that the dial test indicator – often referred to on industrial drawings as a D.T.I. – is not a tool for giving direct readings of size, as will a micrometer or vernier caliper gauge, it is purely and simply a comparator and although it is sometimes used for determining linear measurements up to its operating range, this is not the purpose for which it was designed nor will the manufacturers claim a high degree of linear accuracy over its entire operating range. However, if used with care and discretion it can, in the home workshop, prove to be a useful addition to the metrology department.

CHAPTER 6

Angular Measurement

Measuring angles is one of the most difficult of all measuring operations that the model engineer has to face. Even in industry angular measurement represents a major problem and very sophisticated instruments and equipment have been devised to try to bring about a solution. Fortunately in the home workshop two things are in our favour, firstly, accurate angular measurement is rarely called for and, secondly, as outlined elsewhere in this book, since parts and then mating parts are produced in the same workshop and by the same person, the need for the high degree of accuracy that interchangeability demands is largely eliminated.

As all schoolchildren know, angles are measured in degrees, of which a full circle is 360. These degrees are subdivided into 60 parts called minutes, and each minute is subdivided into a further 60 parts called seconds. Thus, one second is a very small angle indeed, much smaller than anything we are likely to be called upon to consider. The basic instrument for measuring angles is the protractor and in its simplest form this consists of a semi-circle, or sometimes a full circle, of transparent plastic into which lines have been engraved at one degree intervals. This

type of protractor is intended primarily for use in the drawing office or schoolroom where it can be laid down flat on a sheet of paper and used to ascertain the angles of existing lines, or to produce new angles by making a mark at the appropriate engraving around the outer edge. It does not have much practical use in the workshop although the author has known occasions when mutilated bits of these "instruments" have found their way into makeshift appliances − but not where a high degree of accuracy has been required.

The most basic, and by far the most used, of all workshop angular measuring tools is the try-square. This is in fact a protractor permanently set at 90°. Squares come in all types and sizes but for the home workshop the term "square" refers to the engineers' square. This consists of two pieces of material permanently fixed together and called the 'stock' and the 'blade'. The stock is the short heavy leg and the blade is the thin slender leg and both pieces are made of precision ground steel, the blade usually being hardened and tempered. They are made in many sizes but the most useful for our purposes is one with a blade length of about 6in. This size is small enough to be

Fig.48a. This shows the author's well-used 'collection' of squares; the largest one is a 6", the smallest one a minimal 4", the other is an example of an 'adjustable' square. The latter has two blades — one being calibrated. It has proved to be a very useful tool but where maximum accuracy is required the normal fixed blade square is preferred.

Fig.48b. It is important to grip the square firmly when in use otherwise the side load imparted by the scriber may cause the square to move, resulting in an incorrect line. Note that the square is gripped between the thumb and the second, third and fourth fingers, The first finger applies a downward pressure to keep the blade in contact with the workpiece.

used on our relatively small machine tools but still large enough to be able to be used when marking-out the larger items encountered, such as locomotive frames. In use it is normal practice to place the stock onto the datum feature and the blade onto the face being checked or marked.

The square should always be treated with respect; do not drop it down onto the bench so that it runs the risk of being bruised by contacting other objects such as files or hammers, and do not drop it on the floor! If an accident should occur and it does get dropped check to see if any permanent damage has been done. The method for checking is simple and quick. Select a piece of sheet metal with one edge flat and straight. Place the stock of the square firmly up to this edge with the blade facing to the right and scribe a line on the metal using the outer edge of the blade as a guide. Then turn the square over so that the blade now faces towards the left and check to see if the line just

Fig.49 Showing the try-square in use on the surface table. It is of course important to keep the stock of the square in full contact with the table. As one must be kept free for the scriber, holding the workpiece and square must be performed by the other hand and this may represent a problem! The marked line on the illustrated workpiece could be produced more easily by rotating the workpiece 90° and using a scribing block.

scribed is coincident with the outer edge of the blade. If it is, then the square is accurate and all is well. It is a good idea to periodically check squares for accuracy since a square that is not accurate is of little use and will only lead to problems or even to a scrapped component. In use it is imperative that the stock of the square be kept rigidly held against the datum edge of the workpiece, particularly when using it for marking-out purposes, because when scribing down the edge of the blade a force will be applied to the blade by the scriber which will tend to move the stock from contact with the datum face, resulting in an out-of-square line.

The workshop protractor is similar to the try-square except that the blade can be moved and set to any angle by means of a graduated scale. Once set it is then used in the same way as the try-square. If this fact is kept in mind then it will greatly help the user, and applying a protractor to a workpiece will present no problems. There are a number of types of protractor available. The simplest of engineer's protractors is shown in fig.50 and consists of a steel blade and a head that is graduated in degrees – usually from zero to 180°. The blade can be pivoted about a central screw which incorporates a locking device to enable the blade to be set in any desired position. A protractor of this type will be adequate for most of the angular measurement the model engineer will meet although a high degree of accuracy cannot be expected from a tool of this type.

One of the main problems with protractors is their relatively small size. For ease of handling they must be kept to a reasonable size. If it were possible for the scale to be 12in. or so in diameter, then each degree marking would be about 1/10in., apart and at this size it would be possible to subdivide each degree into, say, four parts thus giving a reading in increments of 15 minutes. However, a tool of this size would be impractical to use and would certainly be useless in the small amateur workshop. The usual size for a protractor scale is about 3in. diameter and at this size the distance between the degree markings is in the order of .025in.

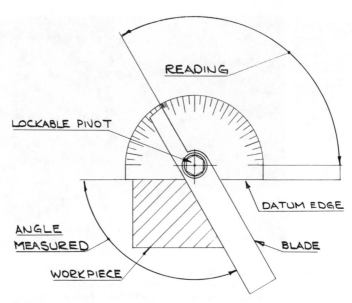

Fig.50 Showing a simple basic engineering protractor.

and since it is not practical to subdivide this further this means that one degree is the smallest increment that can be obtained by direct reading.

Often the length over which the angle is considered is much larger than the size of the protractor dial. On a locomotive frame or traction engine hornplate, for example, the considered distance could be 10 inches or so and one degree over this distance represents almost 3/16in. of linear displacement. It can be seen from this, therefore, that the greater the length over which the angle is considered, the greater the linear discrepancy for a given angular error. Which illustrates the comment made in the first paragraph of this chapter that angular measurement can give rise to problems in the workshop. One way of reducing the possible error is to try to obtain a more accurate reading of the instrument scale and this can be

achieved by providing the protractor with a vernier scale. Most of the protractors available are graduated from 0°-90° reading in two directions and it therefore follows that it will be necessary for any vernier scale fitted to have the facility to be also read in both directions. In actual fact the vernier attachment is a single plate with two distinct scales based on a common zero. The range of each scale is usually 12 divisions which means that each division is 1/12 of a degree, or 5 minutes. It is, therefore, possible with a vernier protractor to set the instrument to within 5 minutes which represents a linear displacement over 10 inches of about .015in. – an improvement over the standard protractor. The 12 divisions of the vernier scale are made equal to 23 divisions of the main scale and not 11 as might be expected. The reason for this is the close proximity to each other of the

THE VERNIER PROTRACTOR SCALE SET
AT ZERO. THE 'O' AND BOTH 60 LINES
ON THE VERNIER SCALE COINCIDE WITH
A MAIN SCALE LINE

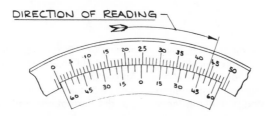

DIRECTION OF READING

SHOWING A READING OF $24° + 45' + 5' = 24°·50'$
THERE IS ONLY ONE LINE ON THE VERNIER
SCALE IN THE DIRECTION OF READING THAT
COINCIDES WITH A LINE ON THE MAIN SCALE

Fig.51 Showing the vernier scale applied to a protractor.

degree divisions would make the vernier scale difficult to read if it were based on 11 divisions of the main scale. This does not in any way alter the basic principle of the vernier scale, it just means that one vernier division is $1/12°$, or 5 minutes, shorter than two scale divisions. The reading of the scale is not affected or altered at all other than it is easier to read owing to the scale being twice as large.

If the application of the vernier scale to the protractor is considered to be the same as the vernier scale on the caliper gauge, it will be quickly and readily understood. It is not in any way necessary to memorise the principles involved in the vernier when using it, but it does help if the operator knows why and how it functions. When reading the vernier protractor first note the number of whole degrees on the main scale then, reading in the same direction and starting at zero on the ver-

Fig.52a. A modern high quality protractor fitted with magnifying lens.

nier scale, count the number of spaces to a line on the vernier which coincides to a line on the main scale. For each of these divisions add on 5 minutes. The vernier scale is itself calibrated, usually in incre-

ments of 15 minutes, so the maximum number of lines to be counted is only two! As outlined above, the vernier scale is in fact two scales; it is vitally important to use the correct one and this is always the

Fig.52b. Gauging small angles by means of a small protractor can be very difficult; to over- come this the tool shown in the previous photograph has an acute angle attachment. This adjustable attachment is shown fitted to the protractor in this illustration. The vernier scale can also be clearly seen in the magnifying lens.

scale in the direction of the reading. Fig.51 shows diagrammatically a vernier protractor scale showing a reading of 24°-50'. The photograph, fig.52, illustrates a modern bevel protractor which has the additional aid of a magnifying screen fitted to the vernier scale.

Where a great degree of angular accuracy has to be achieved, some means other than a protractor must be used. It was described how an error of one degree over 10 inches would result in a linear error approximately 3/16in. If, therefore, the angle required can be expressed as a linear displacement at some known distance from the point of intersection, and this displacement be measured to even a coarse tolerance, say with a rule, the resulting angle obtained will be to a higher degree of accuracy than that obtained with the ordinary protractor. If the linear size is capable of being measured to within approximately .001 of an inch then an exceedingly accurate angle can be produced.

THE SINE BAR

The tool which engineers use to determine angles, using the above method, is called the sine bar. It is an accurate parallel steel bar with two identical rollers attached at a definite centre distance. This distance can vary depending on the size of the workpiece involved but usually the centre distance is either 10in. or 5in. Fig.53 shows a sketch of a typical sine bar. It was the author's intention when starting out to compile this book, to keep mathematics out of it as far as possible but unfortunately should any reader wish to use the sine bar, or the principle involved, then he must resort to the use of simple trigonometrical tables, or at least to the table listing the sines of angles.

If the reader is not familiar with trigonometry it is still possible to use the sine bar and sine tables to obtain an angle without having to make a study of triangles or their trigonometrical function. Refer to fig.54 – here we see a sine bar with one end resting on a flat surface such as a surface plate ad the other end resting on a packing. The sine bar is now at an angle to the surface plate. Since the length of the sine bar remains constant it follows that if we alter the size of the packing it will also alter the angle. In other words, the size of the packing will determine the angle, or, to put it the other way round, the angle required will determine the size of the packing needed. Now, if we divide the size of the packing by the length of the sine bar we get a figure – always less than one – and this figure is called the sine of the angle. It is a simple as that!

Many workshop manuals, and certainly all books on trigonometric functions, contain a table of sines, and this table lists side-by-side the figure obtained by dividing the height of the packing by the length of the sine bar, with the angle which corresponds to this figure. If, therefore, we know the angle but do not know the sine, look down the list of angles until the required figure is revealed and simply read off the sine. If the sine is known but the angle is not, look down the sine column and read off the angle. For example, supposing we require to know the size of the packing required to give an angle of 20°. The table of sines for 20° gives a figure of .342, now this is the figure we get when the size of the packing is divided by the length of the sine bar, so if we multiply the length of the sine bar – which is 5in. – by the .342, we shall obtain the size of the packing, i.e. .342 x 5in. = 1.710in. It is now apparent why 5in. was chosen for the sine bar length, it is very easy to multiply by 5 – simply divide

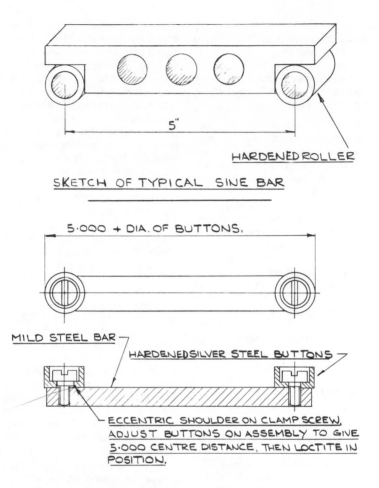

SKETCH OF TYPICAL SINE BAR

5·000 + DIA. OF BUTTONS.

MILD STEEL BAR

HARDENED SILVER STEEL BUTTONS

ECCENTRIC SHOULDER ON CLAMP SCREW, ADJUST BUTTONS ON ASSEMBLY TO GIVE 5·000 CENTRE DISTANCE, THEN LOCTITE IN POSITION.

Fig.53 Sine bars– The upper view shows a typical commercial example. The lower views suggest how the amateur can produce his own bars.

by 2 and move the decimal point one place! It is just as simple working from the packing size to obtain the angle. Supposing the packing measures 1.545in., if we divide this by 5in. we get the figure .309; looking up this number in the table of sines gives the answer 18°. The advent of the electronic pocket calculator has made the process much easier as the engineering or scientific calculators contain in their memory all the trigonometrical functions including the sines. So, using one of these instruments will give you, at the press of a button, the value of the sine, and by pressing another button will perform the multiplication or division for you. Since ac-

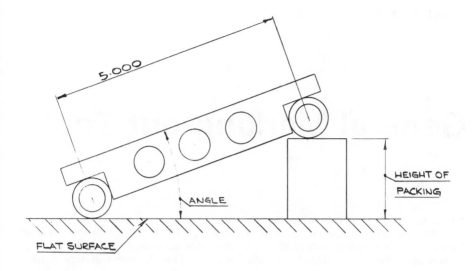

$$\frac{\text{HEIGHT OF PACKING}}{\text{LENGTH OF SINE BAR}} = \text{SINE OF ANGLE}$$

$$\text{TO FIND ANGLE :-} \quad \text{SINE OF ANGLE} = \frac{\text{HEIGHT OF PACKING}}{5}$$

$$\text{TO FIND HEIGHT OF PACKING :-} \quad 5 \times \text{SINE OF ANGLE}$$

Fig.54 Showing the principle of the sine bar.

quiring one of these calculators the author has left the book of tables permanently in the book rack!

Once the basic idea behind the sine bar has been understood then this knowledge can be used in general marking-out practice for obtaining accurate angles. It will be obvious from the above that obtaining accurate angles with the protractors the amateur is likely to possess is, to say the least, hazardous. If these angles can be set out as triangles and the length of the sides measured – even with a steel rule –

then angles obtained by this method will meet the demands of any workpiece likely to be produced in the home workshop. This is not to suggest that all protractors should be disregarded, far from it, they are useful pieces of equipment and a considerable asset to the workshop equipment. However, there are also times when only a slight knowledge of basic mathematics is in itself a considerable force in one's armoury when facing the variety of challenges that the workshop can present.

CHAPTER 7

General Marking-out Tools

All the tools that have been discussed so far have had one factor in common, they have all been measuring devices of some form or other that have enabled a specific distance to be determined from one point or face to another point or face. The measurements have been in a straight line and therefore in one dimension only. All the components that will be produced or measured in the workshop will be three-dimensional — although the marking-out on plate work will be done in two planes only, so this type of work may be considered as two-dimensional. Before any work can be carried out on a component it will be necessary to 'mark-out' that component and for this certain tools will be required.

SURFACE PLATES

In some cases it is an advantage, and in other cases essential, that some flat surface be used as a datum for the marking-out process, the component being placed upon the flat surface whilst the marking-out process is performed. Special flat and true surfaces are produced for this purpose called 'Surface Plates' and these are an important and necessary piece of workshop equipment. Surface plates are produced commercially in two grades, 'A' and 'B', with the 'A' grade surface being the more accurate and also the more expensive. The 'A' grade surface plate is finished by hand scraping and, size for size, will cost about twice as much as a 'B' grade plate which will have a machine ground finish. They are made in all sizes ranging from about 6-inches by 4-inches up to 12-feet by 6-feet or even larger. As it would not be practical to place the larger sizes on a work bench, they are fitted with legs and are free-standing. These are referred to as surface tables or marking-out tables. The larger sizes of these tables are often made from granite and a black granite surface table is the ultimate datum standard. Nature has produced this material which, when finished-machined, will give a long lasting wear-resistant surface which is not only stress-free and rigid but which is also unaffected by magnetic influences and most chemical actions. However, this type of datum surface is usually well outside the scope of the amateur workshop not only because of its physical size but also because of its extreme weight and cost!.

The cast-iron surface plate is perfectly satisfactory for the amateur workshop

Fig.55 This shows a cast-iron surface plate 8" x 6". A plate smaller than this would have a limited use. Most plates are fitted with carrying or lifting handles as shown.

although the author has found that the smaller sizes, such as 6-inches by 4-inches, are too small for general marking-out purposes, as once the workpiece— such as a casting – is placed upon it there is no room left for the marking equipment. Cast-iron is a good material for our type of surface plate because it can readily be made flat (or at least flat enough for our needs) and is hard enough to withstand wear from the rubbing action of tools, etc. Also, the free graphite present in cast-iron helps to make it self-lubricating thus allowing tools such as surface gauges to slide freely over it.

In order to prevent a rocking action, surface plates are fitted with only three feet which enables them to sit firmly on a bench top that may leave a little to be desired with regard to flatness. They are also, with the possible exception of the very small surface plates, rigidly webbed on the underside, thus reducing the tendency to warp or twist. Figs.55 and 56 show both the top and underside of two surface plates.

Fig.56 The underside of a cast-iron surface plate. Note how it is webbed to give added rigidity. The three supporting feet are also clearly seen.

The surface plate is not only used as a datum for marking-out items, it is also a flat reference surface and can be used for checking the flatness of a machined component such as a port-face of a cylinder casting. If the surface of the plate is coated with a fine coloured marking medium, the port-face of the casting can be placed face down onto it and gently rubbed in a circular motion. The high spots on the port-face will 'pick-up' the coloured marker and will indicate just where to remove the metal with the scraper. Red lead and thin oil will make a good marking fluid, but most engineers' stores sell a commercial product sometimes called 'engineers' marking blue' or 'dispersion blue', and, certainly, blue seems to be a good colour for this purpose. However, a word of advice — whatever marker is used it must be used very sparingly otherwise the gap between the surface plate and the workpiece will be bridged by the marker and a completely false marking obtained. Do not use a lapping compound between the surface plate and component as this will destroy the accuracy of the surface plate. In fact, if the workpiece is of a soft material, such as bronze or gunmetal, small pieces of the abrasive will become embedded into the softer material and lap away the surface plate!

The author has found that a surface plate about 8-inches by 6-inches is a satisfactory size for the home or small workshop when it is being used as a datum for checking or obtaining flat surfaces, but even this size is far too restrictive for general marking-out practices. Marking-out is made far more difficult if the operator is having to work in cramped conditions but, as already discussed, larger plates are heavy and in most cases well outside the price restrictions that are of necessity imposed on the amateur, or even school workshops. Fortunately there is a cheap and simple solution, as a very effective marking-out plate can be made from a piece of plate glass. This material is flat to within limits that are perfectly acceptable to the model engineer. It does have a tendency, if not supported, to bend to quite an alarming degree but this can be overcome by placing the plate glass onto a stout wooden base — chipboard is perfectly satisfactory — and the author has also found that a few sheets of paper between the board and the glass is a distinct improvement.

However, this type of surface plate does have its drawbacks in that it has to be treated with great care so as not to break it — but it can be argued that any ill-treatment that would lead to the glass breaking would quite probably have caused permanent damage to a genuine surface plate! Since glass is relatively cheap this type of 'surface plate' can also be used as a lapping plate without the fear of destroying the accuracy of an expensive piece of equipment and if, after a while, the glass becomes hollow as a result of long lapping sessions it is a simple matter to replace it — but do not forget to turn the glass over and use the other side first! Before leaving surface plates, one final thought: they are not anvils and hammering and straightening bent workpieces should not be carried out on any surface plate — particularly a glass one!

SCRIBERS

If accurate marking-out is to be undertaken then it is important that a good quality scriber should be used. All too often the amateur has but little regard for his scriber and uses it for a poker, tommy bar, or even a punch, with the result that the scriber begins to resemble a bent nail

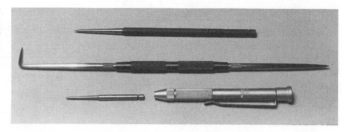

Fig.57 Three engineers' scribers. The lower one has removable points, which is an advantage as any number of points can be used in the one body, including tungsten carbide points.

and, as far as marking-out is concerned, is about as much use as one. Do not forget that it is this tool that produces the lines that mark the boundaries of a component and if the scribing is poor then it will be difficult to work to the line – and this could lead to spoiled components. The scribed line should be bold, thin and not very deep and it is therefore important to have a good scriber and a sharp one. Even with modern prices, scribers are not expensive tools, so when purchasing one make sure you get a good quality product.

The point of a scriber is the most important feature as this is the functional part of the tool. In use the point is very highly stressed and so to give good service and long life it must be hard but not brittle, otherwise it will crumble under the load. For what appears to be such a simple tool it is surprising how large a selection is commercially available, although there are only a few basic patterns. The simplest scribers are produced from a single piece of steel about 3/16in. diameter and about $4\frac{1}{2}$in. long. They are pointed at one end only and knurled for most of their length. The knurling is to provide a firm grip for the fingers during use. This type of scriber is sometimes referred to as a machinist's scriber and one is illustrated in the photograph (fig.57). Another single-piece scriber is the engineer's bent or right-angled scriber and this is similar to the previous one except

that there is a point at both ends, one of which is bent over at right-angles. This bent portion is handy for getting into awkward places. The main objection the author has to these two scribers is that they cannot, with safety, be carried around in the pocket; however, if they are kept in a drawer or cupboard close to where they are going to be used then there is no need to carry them around. It is advisable to protect the point when not in use, a cork or similar device pushed over the end not only protects the points but also eliminates the risk of inadvertently jabbing one's hand on what is a very sharp point.

The most popular type of scriber is the one with removable points, and these are called pocket or toolmakers' scribers. The main body of this type of scriber is produced from a free cutting steel and is in fact a handle into which the scriber point fits, the point being held in place by means of a small screwed collet. This type of scriber has advantages over the one-piece tool in that only the scriber point itself is made from tool steel and as these are small, simple items the cost of replacement is relatively small; also, after use, the point can be reversed in the holder, thus protecting both point and user. A number of points can be kept for the one holder including tungsten carbide ones. This is an extremely hard material, much harder than the tool steel, and so

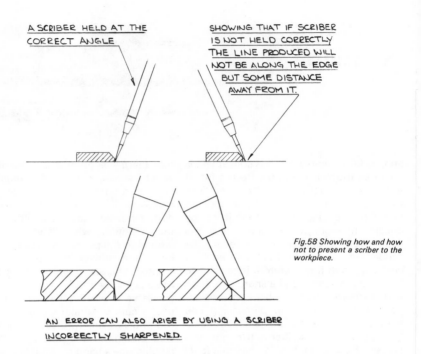

A SCRIBER HELD AT THE
CORRECT ANGLE

SHOWING THAT IF SCRIBER
IS NOT HELD CORRECTLY
THE LINE PRODUCED WILL
NOT BE ALONG THE EDGE
BUT SOME DISTANCE
AWAY FROM IT.

Fig.58 Showing how and how not to present a scriber to the workpiece.

AN ERROR CAN ALSO ARISE BY USING A SCRIBER
INCORRECTLY SHARPENED.

this type of point is ideal for work on castings where the hard sandy surface can quickly blunt the tool steel point. (Fig.57 shows a scriber of this type).

In use the scriber is held in a similar way to a pencil, for it is after all a drawing instrument. When using the scriber with a rule or straight edge as a guide, the point of the scriber must be tilted in towards the guide, as failure to do this could result in a marked line not being along the edge of the guide but some distance away from it. If a second pass is then made along the straight edge the chances are that a double line may be the result. The diagram, fig.58, illustrates this point.

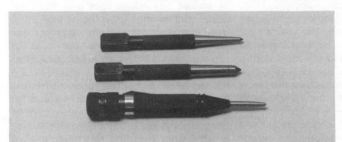

Fig.59 This shows three commercial punches. The top one, being of small diameter, can be used as a dot or prick punch, the middle punch being larger can be used for providing the 'start' for a drill. The lower punch is an automatic punch and can be used in place of the 'dot' punch.

CENTRE PUNCHES

As the name implies this tool is used for marking a point to locate the centre of a hole that has to be drilled. In marking-out this is usually at the intersection of two scribed lines. It is not practical to start a normal twist drill in the desired spot without giving the drill some form of guide, and this guide is the indentation made by the centre punch. This mark is usually referred to as the 'centre pop'. If the hole centre has been accurately marked then in order to maintain this accuracy a good true 'pop' mark at the exact intersection of the line is essential. It therefore follows that good quality punches, well maintained and correctly used, are required. It is recommended that two punches be available in the workshop, one about 1/8in. diameter at the top of the cone point, the other being larger, say about 3/16in. diameter. The conical point of the smaller punch should be ground to an included angle of about 60° and this type of punch is usually referred to as a 'dot' punch. The cone angle on the larger punch, which is the actual centre punch, should be about 90° inclusive. Both types of punch are available commercially and are listed in manufacturers' catalogues as dot and centre punches respectively.

The dot punch should be the first punch to be used. Since it is smaller in diameter and is generally a slimmer version of the centre punch, it is easier to locate the line intersection with the dot punch, also the indentation made will be smaller in diameter owing to the narrower angle. This is just the type of 'pop' required for locating the points of dividers used for scribing radii or setting out dimensions. If a hole has to be drilled then the larger punch is used to open out the indentation. It is a simple matter to accurately locate the larger punch in the hole produced by the dot punch. A drill started in the 90° indentation has a better chance of remaining in the true position than it would have in the original dot punch hole.

The punches themselves have to be made from a good quality tool steel as the pointed end has to be hardened and tempered. The remainder of the punch, particularly the top, must be tough enough to withstand the hammer blows. As in the case of the scribers, the shank of the punch is usually knurled to provide a good fingergrip. Some manufacturers produce punches with a square section head, which does not alter the effectiveness of the punch in any way but it does prevent it from rolling off the bench top and magically disappearing under the bench! Spring loaded 'automatic' dot punches are produced which do not need a hammer blow to produce the indentation. The body of this type of punch is hollow and contains a spring and striker mechanism. The punch is placed on the workpiece and steady downward pressure applied on the body compresses the spring until the striker is automatically released and the resultant blow is applied to the punch point. The tension of the spring can be adjusted by rotating the punch body thus allowing the size of the blow to be varied; all the marks made at any one setting with this type of punch will be of uniform size. The photograph, fig.59, shows various types of centre punches.

It is not particularly easy to produce the 'pop' mark just where it is required. If the lines have been produced by means of a sharp scriber and the dot punch is as sharp as it should be then it is possible to feel the point of the punch into the line intersection; the use of a magnifying glass may also be helpful. Only lightly dot the work at first, then carefully examine the result. If the dot is where is should be then

Fig.60 Showing the recommended way of holding a centre punch; it is firmly held between the thumb and three fingers, the little finger providing a support for the point so preventing it from moving out of position whilst a light hammer blow is being applied.

it is a simple matter to apply the punch a second time to obtain the depth required for either producing a start for a drill, or location of a divider point. Should the dot be out of position then the punch will have to be angled for the second blow to 'throw' the dot over to its correct position.

Most faulty punch marks are a result of incorrectly holding the punch. To get the dot in the correct position first time it is essential to hold the punch vertically – if the punch is angled then the dot will move over in the direction of inclination. It is also important to have complete control over the punch; it must be firmly held and supported whilst the blow is being applied. The punch should be held between the thumb and second finger with the first finger supporting the head of the punch. The tip of the third finger should be steadying the punch point and at the same time resting on the workpiece. The photograph, fig.60, il-

lustrates this. The hammer used should only be a light one, certainly no more than a half-pound, lighter if possible.

DIVIDERS

The names of many tools define the work they perform and in this respect dividers are no exception. One of their uses is to divide a line into a number of equal parts. This is done by the trial and error method of guessing the distance required and then, from the starting point, stepping out the number of divisions wanted – hoping to finish at the predetermined position. It is most unlikely that this will be achieved first time so the dividers are adjusted and another attempt made. Three or four tries should be sufficient to arrive at the correct divider setting. There are, however, other ways of dividing a line into a number of equal parts and there are also other duties that can be accomplished by a pair of dividers. Their main duty is to provide a means of marking arcs and circles from a

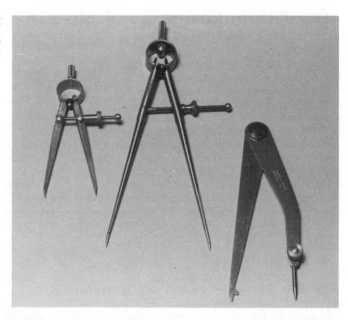

predetermined centre and, as such, dividers are really a special form of scriber. Another use for dividers is that of transferring dimensions from a rule to the workpiece. When doing this, do not use the end of the rule for a datum – as is done with calipers – but place one leg of the dividers in the one-inch graduation and then adjust the distance between the legs until the second leg clicks into the rule division required. Do not forget, however, to allow for the one-inch of the rule that is not being used. Failure to do so is most unlikely with small distances but with larger dimensions any error may not be so obvious.

Dividers are very similar in construction to calipers although nowadays they are all of the spring-bow type. However, dividers have a small knurled knob protruding from the centre line of the bowspring to allow the divider to be rotated between the thumb and first finger. Spring bow instruments of all types are inclined to flex under load and once the load is removed the legs go back to their original position. If, therefore, a pair of spring bow dividers is driven round by the legs rather than by the special knurled knob provided, the chances are that the setting of the dividers will vary slightly during the marking operation and an incorrect line will be scribed. A second pass with the dividers may then lead to a double line – and neither may be correct! When the points are close together springing and flexing of the legs becomes a problem and it is therefore advisable to have two pairs of dividers in the workshop, a 6-inch set and a 3-inch set, the smaller ones naturally being used for the smaller radii. The size of a pair of dividers is obtained by measuring the distance between the pivot centre and the bottom of the legs.

71

HERMAPHRODITE CALIPERS

In the workshop these are usually referred to as 'odd legs' or 'jenny legs' and, as the name implies, they are similar to dividers and calipers except the legs are odd. In fact, one leg is similar to the leg of an inside caliper, the other leg is similar to a divider leg.

Their main use is for scribing a line parallel to a datum edge. The caliper leg is placed against the datum edge and with the opening of the legs set to the desired size, the scriber leg is drawn along the workpiece. This will produce a line parallel to, or equally distant from, the datum edge. It is essential, of course, to keep the caliper leg in contact with the datum edge throughout the entire length of the scribed line and in order to help achieve this, the caliper leg on some makes of hermaphrodite calipers is provided with a locating spur set at right angles to the leg and about 3/16in. or so from the bottom. This spur rides along the top face of the datum edge and prevents this leg from moving vertically up and down the datum. This is important because any vertical movement of the caliper leg will affect the position of the line from the datum edge and result in an incorrectly marked line. In fact, is advisable, when buying this type of caliper, to make sure that it is provided with the spur (fig.61 shows quite clearly).

Another use for odd legs is locating the centre of the bar and this is done by setting the legs at about half the diameter of the bar and placing the spur on the cylindrical face. An arc is drawn on the end face, then three more arcs are drawn at approximately 90° intervals and it will then be apparent from the four arcs where the centre is located. This, however, is not really a precision way of centre locating, nor one that the author makes a practice of using.

Odd legs are, as a rule, firm jointed and are nearly always fitted with removable and adjustable scribing points. It will be appreciated from the above that this type of caliper can only be used from a datum edge and is of little use when marking out a sheet from a datum line.

TRAMMELS

It will be apparent from the discussion on dividers that they have limitations with regard to size, since the longer the legs become the more they begin to lose rigidity and the more unwieldy they are to use. They are actually produced commercially up to a size of 12 inches, but using dividers of this size is, to say the least, an experience. Therefore, some other way of producing the larger arcs, say 6 inches and above, is desirable and the ideal tool for this task is a set, or a pair, of trammels. A set of trammels consists of two movable heads and a rigid beam. The heads are the means of securing scriber points but as they also have to be able to move alongthe beam to establish a setting they must be provided with a locating and locking device. Unfortunately, the author does not know of any manufacturers now producing small trammel sets that are suitable for amateur or model engineering workshops. On the other hand, however, they are not difficult to make and the little time their construction would take will prove well worthwhile, particularly if the constructor wishes to build the larger type of model.

The beam could be made from a piece of bright drawn mild steel. Square section could be used as this would then ensure that the heads maintain vertical alignment; alternatively, the beam could be produced from circular rod with vertical alignment maintained by machining a flat over the entire length of the beam. Certainly the heads would be easier to make if the beam were circular, as a drilled hole presents far less of a problem to produce than a square hole. If the clamping screw for locking the head to the beam used the flat for its contact face, automatic alignment of the heads would take place when these screws were tightened. The actual scriber points – which could be the commercial points supplied for the pocket-type scriber – could be secured to the head either by a locking-type collet or clamp screw. A refinement would be to eccentrically mount one of the scriber points as fine adjustment could then be made by rotating this point.

Inexperienced users will soon find that trammels are easy tools to use. This is mainly due to their inherent stability. The scriber points are in close proximity to the beams and the whole tool is only about an inch or so above the workpiece. Both hands are needed to use the trammels – one on each head. With right-handed users, the left hand is the anchor hand, the circular motion being applied with the right hand. This results in the downward pressure being almost directly over the scriber points and so very little bending moment is given to the beam. This, in turn, eliminates any tendency for the scriber points to spread under load. In fact, providing the anchor scriber is sitting in a good and well-formed 'pop' made with a dot punch, it is possible to go over the same scribed line a number of times without the risk of doubling or spreading the line.

COMBINATION SETS OR SQUARES

Tools that claim to be able to perform a large variety of functions are more often than not of little use. They rarely perform any function well and are best left severe-ly alone by the serious worker. However, the combination set is an exception to this rule and is a very useful addition to the workshop equipment. Generally a combination set consists of four pieces – the rule, the square head, the protractor and the centre head.

The basis of the set is the rule, this being a 12-inch or 300mm rigid square-ended rule, thicker than the ordinary rule and with a keyway or slot down the centre of one face running the complete length of the rule. As an individual item it can obviously be used as a rule or straight-edge. The other three items can in turn have the rule inserted into them with the keyway locating and guiding them into position. A locking screw secures each item in any desired position along the length of the rule. When the square head is used the tool does in fact become a try-square with an available blade length of 12 inches. As the rule can be set to give any required projection from the face of the square, It can also be used as a depth gauge, although some restrictions will be encountered owing to the rule being in the region of one inch wide. However, it can be used for obtaining, or checking, depths of steps or flanges. The square head is also fitted with a 45° face and a spirit level, the latter being useful in setting things parallel to the surface plate, providing of course that the surface plate is itself set level. The blade in the square head is also useful on the surface plate as it will stand with the rule in the vertical position thus permitting distance above the surface plate to be obtained.

The protractor head naturally turns the tool into a protractor – again with a 12-inch blade, although its use in this form is limited, particularly when set at shallow angles.

The centre square is intended for deter-

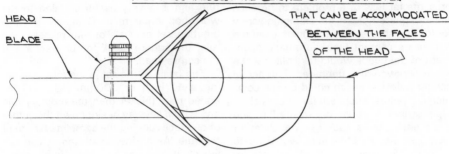

A LINE SCRIBED ALONG THIS EDGE OF THE BLADE
WILL PASS THROUGH THE CENTRE OF ANY DIAMETER
THAT CAN BE ACCOMMODATED
BETWEEN THE FACES
OF THE HEAD

HEAD

BLADE

Fig.62 The centre square

mining the centre position of square or round stock. The head is arranged so that the blade bisects the angle between the 90° face of the square so that when applied to a circular object, one edge of the rule will pass through the centre position.

By doing this in two places, the point where the lines intersect is the centre of the circle (see fig.62).

CHAPTER 8

Tools for Marking Castings, Forgings etc

In addition to the tools so far examined, further appliances will be needed if successful marking and measuring of castings and similar components is to be undertaken. What we are now looking for is some means of determining and marking points or lines in the vertical plane above the datum or face-plate.

SURFACE GAUGE

As with other types of marking, the line required on the workpiece can be made by means of a scriber and therefore all that is wanted is a means of holding the scriber at any pre-determined distance above the datum face, coupled with the facility of being able to move the scriber along or around the workpiece. The tool that meets these conditions is called the surface gauge or scribing block. In its simplest form it consists of a relatively heavy and robust base into which is mounted a vertical column. A special scriber is secured to the column by means of a clamp which is so arranged that the one knurled headed clamp screw will lock both the clamp to the column and the scriber to the clamp. It is possible to rotate the scriber about the clamp screw, thus enabling fine adjustments to be made to the height of the scriber. If the clamp screw is partially

slackened, the clamp will not readily move up and down the column but it will be possible to move the scriber against a slight resistance until the correct setting is obtained. The clamp screw can then be tightened and both scriber and clamp firmly secured. Two holes are usually provided in the clamp screw sleeve at right-angles to one another, a small one about 1/8in. diameter for the scriber and a larger hole suitable for accepting dial indicators.

This simple form of scribing block can easily be made in the small or home workshop and in order to assist any constructor the clamp block, screw and sleeve are shown in fig.63. The scriber can be made from a piece of 1/8in. diameter silver steel but before hardening and tempering, make it double-ended and bend one end over as shown in the photographs. This bent end allows the scribing block to be used for positioning work parallel to the surface plate and, of course, it can also be used for setting workpieces in machine tools.

The universal type of surface gauge is illustrated in fig.64, and, as can be seen, is more sophisticated than the simple scribing block. The base is rectangular with the underface machined and scraped true and

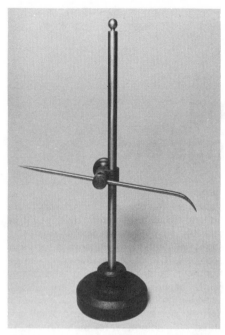

Fig.63 This is a simple form of scribing block. It is not difficult for the amateur to make his own although the one illustrated is a commercially available tool. The larger hole visible in the sleeve is for securing a dial test indicator.

flat. It also has a 'V' groove machined across its length which allows the gauge to be accurately located onto cylindrical workpieces. Also incorporated in the base are two retractable guide pegs. When these are withdrawn downwards they can be placed into contact with a machined edge of a large workpiece or with the edge of a regular surface plate. The whole gauge can then be slid along the edge and if the pegs are kept in contact with the edge the gauge will then move in a straight line parallel to the datum edge. The author has not found many cases in model engineering where this facility was a great asset!

The pillar of the universal surface gauge is not securely fastened into the base but is held in a cross drilled spindle which can be rotated to allow the pillar to

Fig.64 An example of the universal surface gauge; the various facilities referred to in the text are all visible.

Fig.65 Setting the height of the surface gauge. Supporting the rule as shown will ensure that it is perpendicular to the surface plate. Note the scriber is almost horizontal and there is a minimum of overhang.

be moved from the vertical. This not only helps in the adjustment of the scriber point height but also increases the reach of the scriber should this be desired. Fine height adjustment is made by means of a rocking lever and adjusting screw. The rocking lever is pivoted on the base with the adjusting screw on one end of the lever and the spindle carrying the pillar in the other end. The locking lever is spring-loaded so that it moves by means of the adjusting screw in one direction and by the influence of the spring in the reverse direction. The photograph, fig.64, shows an example of a universal surface gauge.

In use it will not be practical to get lines as deep as can be obtained with the ordinary hand scriber owing to the lack of rigidity in the complete arrangement. With hand scribing, particularly on sheet metal, the workpiece has the complete rigidity of the bench behind it and the pressure is applied almost directly over the scriber point, consequently there is nothing to move or flex. Using a surface gauge on the surface plate is a completely different circumstance. The workpiece on the surface

plate will, by the nature of things, be comparatively small and light and will therefore be able to withstand only the slightest pressure before movement of the workpiece takes place. Certainly, in order to obtain any mark at all the workpiece will have to be held down in some way. The surface gauge is also basically a flimsy tool and one not capable of accepting a great deal of pressure on the scriber point. This does not mean that clear,sharp markings cannot be achieved, they most certainly can, but it does mean that to obtain them the scriber point must be kept in good condition.

To accurately make a mark or line a specific vertical distance above the datum face of the surface plate, it is necessary first of all to set the point of the scriber to the distance required. From the amateur point of view the measuring device used will almost certainly be the rule. There are pitfalls and care must be taken or the setting could be incorrect. In order to obtain a true setting it is essential that the rule used should be set square to the surface plate in both planes. It is also equally important that the datum end of the rule used should be in contact with the surface plate.

It is not possible to achieve these conditions by simply placing the rule on the surface plate and holding it there by hand, and some positive means must be found to guarantee the correct attitude of the rule. It was mentioned earlier when discussing combination squares that if the square is placed on the surface plate it will hold the rule perpendicular to the plate; this is so and if the rule is set so that the square datum end is in contact with the surface plate, satisfactory rule reading can be transferred to the surface gauge. This method can, however, be cumbersome as the square will have the tendency to fall over or move about unless held down. Also for smaller measurements, the actual square shrouds the rule. A satisfactory method is to place the rule onto an angle-plate and let the square end of the rule rest onto the surface plate. Fig.65 shows this operation being performed. It is also advisable to aim to get the scriber near the horizontal rather than at a pronounced angle and to also try to get the minimum of overhang between the scriber point and the clamp bracket. These two last points will increase the rigidity of the whole gauge.

In use, grip the base of the gauge with one hand and slide the whole gauge along the surface plate. While a firm downward pressure should be applied to the gauge, only apply a light pressure in the direction of the scriber point. The other hand may have to be used to hold down the workpiece and prevent it moving as it resists the force of the scriber pressure.

ANGLE PLATES

Many of the tools so far mentioned in this book would be useful additions to the workshop but by no means are they are essential pieces of workshop equipment. The angle-plate is an exception, as very little serious work can be performed without the use of one. Although we are only discussing marking and measuring, many of the tools used to perform these operations will have other and more important roles to play in the general activity

Fig.66 Just three of the author's much-used angle-plates. The large one on the right is a commercial example of the webbed variety. The other two were home-made many years ago and have given good service.

of the workshop and the angle-plate is a good example of this. It will be used on the lathe faceplate in order to provide a surface square to the faceplate and it will be used secured directly onto the lathe boring table; it will also be mounted onto the tables of milling and shaping machines and also used on the drilling machines. All of these facts must be taken into consideration when purchasing a piece of equipment – what is ideal for one application may have limitations when applied to some other duty. As with most things in engineering, it is a case of obtaining a good compromise. Unfortunately there is not just one angle-plate that will meet all the conditions mentioned. A $3\frac{1}{2}$in. lathe will only swing a relatively small angle-plate and this would then not be large enough for other general duties. Certainly the size of the angle-plate required on the marking-out plate would be too large for lathe faceplate duties. Angle-plates are expensive items but unlike many of the measuring tools they can be easily made and even the inexperienced constructor should have no difficulty in producing a perfectly acceptable tool. Although the author has, over the years, managed to collect quite a number of angle-plates from a variety of sources, he still has – and uses – some that were made many years ago. Pieces of 'angle iron' have formed the basis of most of them, and true, this is steel rather than the preferable cast iron of the commercial product, but they still give good service. The method of production is simple; bolt one face of the angle down onto the lathe boring table and with a flycutter, either in the chuck or secured in a holder on the faceplate, take a cut over the upright face until it is cleaned up. Then, with the newly-machined face in contact with the boring table, repeat the process on the se-cond face. This will produce an angle-plate adequate for most of the duties it will be asked to fulfil. Slots can be cut in if desired but a few tapped holes is a good alternative. Do not put the tapped holes in any regular pattern, just drill and tap them to suit the component in hand. It is surprising how quickly sufficient holes will be available to cope with most components without the need for drilling more but, of course, should the need arise then more holes will be available the next time the plate is used.

Commercial angle-plates are produced from iron castings and are machined to fine limits, these limits applying not only to the squareness of the faces but also to their flatness. Most of them are also heat-treated to relieve all stresses and so minimise the risk of distortion. They can be obtained in a variety of sizes from about 4in.x2in.x3in. upwards, to sizes far too large to be of any practical use in the back-garden workshop. The smaller sizes can be obtained either with or without end webs. The webs considerably strengthen the angle-plates and increase their rigidity, this being an advantage when the plate is used for supporting a component while it is being machined. On the marking-off table, the open-ended type of angle-plate is preferable as webs have a habit of getting in the way. It is a greater advantage still if the inside of the angle is machined as well as the outside, as this will give the facility of being able to secure components on the inside of the angle and thus increase the scope of the plate. This type of angle-plate is also advantageous over the webbed type when used on the lathe faceplate. The facility of being able to mount components on the inside will mean that the angle-plate can be positioned nearer the centre of the faceplate, thus allowing a larger angle to

Fig.67 Two special-purpose angle-plates; the one on the left is an adjusting angle-plate and is a very useful tool particularly when used in conjunction with the drilling or milling machine. The other is a box-plate – this type of angle-plate is widely used in industry particularly in jobbing shops but unfortunately its assets do not appear to be realised by the model engineering trade.

be used without fear of it fouling the lathe bed. All commercial angle-plates are provided with slots which are not usually machined but are 'cast' in. The slots provide a means of clamping so that the workpiece can be firmly secured to the plate. Securing bolts pass through the clamp and angle-plate and are fastened by means of a nut. A standard nut will not be large enough to span the slots and also give an adequate bolting face and therefore a large spreader washer will have to be used between the nut and angle-plate to prevent the corners of the nut fouling the edge of the slots. The tapped hole in the home-made angle-plate has the advantage of not requiring nuts!

There is a type of angle-plate known as the box angle-plate and, as its name suggests, this is in the shape of a hollow box with an open bottom. It is accurately machined on all faces so that no matter which face is placed in contact with the surface table, the top is parallel to the surface table and the four sides are square to the table and square to each other. This type of angle-plate is very useful as once

the workpiece has been secured to one face, any of the other five faces may be placed in contact with the surface table so all can be used as datum faces should the need arise. Unfortunately, these box plates do not, at the time of writing, appear to be available commercially in sizes suited to our needs and the one shown in the photograph, fig.67, was made by the author.

There are times, not only in marking out but also in the machining of components, when an angle-plate other than the normal 90° is an advantage. This need is filled by the tilting angle-plate which is similar to the ordinary angle-plate but instead of it being a fixed right-angle, the two surfaces of the plate are pivoted to allow them to be set to any angle from the normal 90° to a position where both faces are parallel to each other. A protractor scale is fitted to assist in setting the angle required and is graduated 0°-90°. Setting an angle to this scale will only give a moderate degree of accuracy and if it is necessary to attain accuracy greater than a half-degree or so, then it is recommended that the angle is set using the sine bar method previously outlined. This type of angle-plate may be used most on the drilling machine as it is surprising just how many holes have to be drilled at an angle to a datum face, particularly on model steam engine cylinders.

It will be seen from the above that it is difficult to advise anyone about to purchase an angle-plate as to what size plate to purchase. On the marking-out table a large angle-plate is of most use while in general machining work the large plate may be too big for the small machine tools available in the amateur workshop. The author finds that the angle-plate he uses most on the marking-out table is one measuring 6¼in. long, 4in. in breadth and 5in. high, but this is on the large side for use on the 3½in. lathe although it is perfectly at home on the table of the vertical milling machine. Perhaps the best advice that can be offered is to buy the largest angle-plate that can be afforded and then make the small ones yourself!

VEE BLOCKS

These are used in the main for supporting cylindrical workpieces both on the marking-out table and also on machine tools. A piece of round bar material when laid down on a flat surface is not stable and can easily be made to roll. If it is clamped down directly onto a machine table it will still not be secure enough to take any but the smallest cutting force before it will begin to move and the reason for this is that there are only two lines of contact, one directly over the other, the first one being between the workpiece and the table and the second one being between the workpiece and the clamp. Holding a bar in this way is also detrimental to the machine table or surface plate as even a small clamping pressure will result in overstressing the table and possibly causing permanent damage in the form of an indentation along the line of contact. The problems, however, are overcome by placing the cylinder in a 'Vee' form slot. This 'vee' is

Fig.68 A selection of much-used vee-blocks, most of which are one of a matching pair. The range of blocks shown is more than adequate to meet all the needs of an amateur workshop.

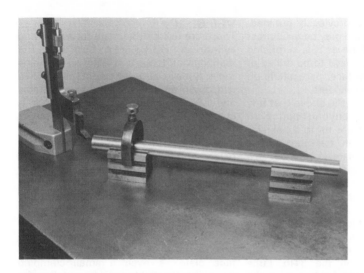

Fig.69a. This shows a shaft resting in a matched pair of vee-blocks. This type of block, which is provided with a clamp, is a very useful tool that can be used in many ways – see fig.70.

machined in a rectangular block of material which is then called a Vee block. If the clamping force is now applied the workpiece will be securely held and the table or surface plate protected from damage because of the large surface area of the underside of the supporting vee block. The workpiece, when clamped in this way, has three points of contact and is therefore stable. The angle of the vee in all general purpose blocks is 90°, 45° either side of the vertical centre line. The bottom corner of the vee is not sharp but is relieved with a small slot, the purpose of

Fig.69b. For a small workpiece only one block may be needed. This photograph also shows a height vernier being used. The height vernier is an alternative way of determining height levels and once its setting has been mastered it is not only more accurate than the surface gauge and rule but also much quicker to use. They are not usually fitted with a scriber point but with a very sharp chisel edge. As can be seen the whole instrument is much more robust in design than the orthodox scribing block and gives very clear concise markings.

this slot being to assist manufacture by eliminating the corner completely. Sharp internal corners are not a practical proposition, or even good design, as not only are they difficult – if not impossible – to produce but they are also notorious stress raisers and should be avoided not only in vee blocks but in design generally.

The larger sizes of vee blocks, those above about 2inches, are usually made from cast iron with the smaller ones made from steel which in most cases is hardened or case-hardened. Although the larger blocks may be made and sold individually, the small blocks are usually produced and sold as matched pairs. In the case of high precision blocks they will be marked and numbered so that they can be identified as a "pair of matched blocks". Fig.68 shows a selection of small sizes of vee blocks.

In order to increase their range the vee shape may be produced on two opposite faces, and in some cases the block may have four vees, each one being of a different size. The larger blocks, which are naturally intended for large and consequently heavy workpieces, will only have one vee and this is necessary in order to obtain the maximum amount of strength to withstand the high stresses they will encounter in general use. It is unlikely that blocks of this type will be of much use in the size of workshop under consideration. The types of vee block the amateur or model engineer will find most useful are those that have two vees, a large one on one side and a small one on the side directly opposite, the other two sides being furnished with grooves or slots which provide a means of locating and receiving a clamp. This type of vee block is shown in the photograph, fig.69. Blocks of this type are commercially available and are usually made from steel and have been heat-treated. The largest of the vee grooves is capable of accepting workpieces of up to about $1\frac{1}{2}$ inches or 40mm diameter. This is large enough for general use in the model engineer's workshop yet also small enough to be used on the small machines found there.

Fig.70 The same workpiece as shown in 69b. The vee-block is now being used to support and hold the workpiece square in the drilling machine.

83

When setting up a small workpiece, say up to about 4in. long, one block may be sufficient to provide the support needed, but for longer workpieces such as shafts then a pair of blocks is recommended. If the blocks are a matched pair and the workpiece is placed in corresponding vees then the shaft will be parallel to the table on which the blocks are resting (fig.69). The ends of the blocks are produced square to the functional faces of the block; if, therefore, the block is placed on a plate or table on one of the ends, a cylindrical workpiece will be set in an upright position square to the reference face, see fig.70.

As was the case with the angle-plate, the vee block will be used more often on a machine tool, particularly a drilling or milling machine, than on the marking-out table and this fact must be kept in mind when choosing a pair of vee blocks.

CHAPTER 9

Marking out Sheet Components and Interpreting Drawings

In the model engineer's workshop the bulk of all marking-out operations will be performed on sheet metal, that is to say, the material will be flat and the shape of the component will be drawn onto the sheet. What in fact the constructor will be doing is copying the details of the component from the drawing and reproducing these onto the metal sheet. The component is then produced by cutting, sawing, filing and drilling to these marked lines. It follows, therefore, that the accuracy of the component will be affected not only by the cutting process but also by the accuracy of the original marking-out and also by the interpretation of the drawing. No matter how accurately, or with what precision, the cutting out is performed, if the marking-out is faulty then the finished component will also be faulty. It pays not to rush into the marking-out process but to take time and care over it. This will be time well spent because to rectify a spoiled component – assuming that rectification is possible – may be much more time-consuming than the whole of the time spent in the marking-out. Even then the final result may not be completely satisfactory.

Before any marking-out is undertaken carefully study the detail drawing of the component and make sure that the function of each individual feature is fully understood. Some of the lines may only mark the boundary of the component and as such do not denote an edge or face that will later make contact with some other piece. Other lines will indicate the position of mating components or be the datum for some other feature. Centres of holes may have to be marked and some of these holes may be tapped whilst some may be clearance holes for bolts or studs and some may even be to locate dowel pins. Other holes, which may not be circular in shape, may be simply to reduce the weight of the component or to provide a means of access to some bolt or feature which on final assembly would otherwise be inaccessible. Whatever the purpose of the feature, make sure that it is fully understood as this could have an effect on the marking-out procedure. Clearly, more care and thought must be given when choosing the correct datum for the location of bolt or dowel holes than when marking some feature such as the outer profile of the component.

The business of fully understanding the nature of the component, what it does and how it functions and what duty it performs in the completed work is far more important in model engineering or general jobbing work than it is in industry. In large industry, particularly those which are now termed multi-nationals, such as the aircraft or automobile industry, the people making any component need no further information than that quoted on the detail drawing. However, that drawing will be a completely different animal to that from which the model engineer has to work. The industrial drawing, which will only give details of one component, will have been prepared, drawn, checked and approved by a team of professionally-trained design engineers and draughtsmen who know full well what is required from the component and all these requirements will be reflected in the final drawing. Every feature will have been dimensioned from its correct datum. Every size will carry a tolerance and these tolerances will not only refer to the linear size but also to their geometric characteristics, surface finish and even the lay of that finish will be called out. Nothing will have been left to chance and it may all have been done with symbols and without a written word, the reason for the latter being that the components may be made in a "foreign" country and by craftsmen who may not speak or understand the language of the draughtsman compiling the drawing.

This type of drawing would be of little use in the amateur's workshop. It would be meaningless to most constructors and even if he could understand the 'shorthand' methods employed on the drawing and had the equipment to meet all the drawing demands, the whole exercise would be pointless. As outlined elsewhere, the reason for high precision is usually to make parts that are interchangeable and will assemble without the need to resort to 'fitting'. One eminent engineer once said that the only thing a fitter made with a file was scrap. While this sentiment most certainly does not apply to the back-garden workshop, it does emphasise the different requirements of modern mass production engineering.

The author is in no way decrying the drawings made both by and for the model engineer but is pointing out how the different methods of manufacture can affect the whole design concept and also the method and techniques required in producing the drawing. Most drawings made for the model engineer or small workshop are produced by a one man 'team'. He will be responsible for the design and presentation and for checking the final product. There is also the model engineer who, having researched and made a model, may be requested to prepare a set of drawings for it. The person concerned may have had no drawing office experience at all, indeed, he may never have had a drawing lesson in his life but considering all the problems that face the model engineer designer, the standard of drawings offered on the market is usually very good. It does pay, however, to study the drawings carefully, not only of the individual component under consideration but also how it fits into the completed assembly, before any metal is cut or marking-out started.

Before the actual marking can commence there may be some preparatory work to be done on the sheet or plate. When drawing with a pencil or pen on paper the line drawn is easily seen, as a black line on a white background is the best condition that can be obtained for contrast between the line and the paper. A scriber only scratches or cuts a line in the material being marked and so will only show as a bright line. To increase the contrast, particularly if bright sheet is being marked, it is recommended that the surface of the sheet be treated with some form of dye. For many years a marking-out medium consisting of copper sulphate dissolved in a very weak nitric acid solution was very popular. When this was applied to bright steel surfaces it turned them copper-coloured, in fact, it gave them a very thin coating of copper which gave a good contrast for the scribed lines. A better, quicker and safer way, however, is to use a modern preparation known as Engineers' Blue Marking Fluid, or Lay-out fluid as it is called by some manufacturers. This is a special dye which when applied to any component gives it a deep blue colour. Only a small amount is needed, a few drops placed on a rag and quickly wiped over the surface of the plate is all that is required and, being spirit based, this dries almost as soon as it is applied.

Measurements are made, or dimensions taken, from one point, face or edge in order to determine the position of some new feature. The starting point for the measurement is referred to as the datum. If, therefore, when marking-out a component onto a piece of sheet metal, two datum edges or lines are established, one at right-angles to the other, then all points relating to every feature can be established by one measurement from each datum. In the case of sheet metal, one datum can be one edge of the sheet, usually the longest, and this edge should be dressed or filed as straight as possible. The datum at right-angles may also be another side of the sheet but this must not only be straight but also square with the first datum and it will need careful dressing to obtain this condition. It is often an advantage not to use an edge for the second datum but to use a scribed line, this line being produced by means of a try-square. The position of the scribed line on the sheet will depend on the shape of the component being marked-out. If the shape is basically rectangular then the scribed datum will be close to one end, but if the component is symmetrical about a centre line then this centre line will become the datum line. This method of positioning all points from two datums at right-angles will eliminate the accumulation of errors that could arise if the measuring were done from point to point. Reference to fig.71a illustrates this. There we see a group of holes and if the position of each hole is measured from the datum edge and the degree of accuracy that can be obtained in each measurement is .005in., then the last hole in a series of five will be within the .005in. error. If, however, the method of marking is to position each hole from its adjacent hole, as in fig.71b, then, since each hole can have a possible error of .005in., the final hole could be .025in. from its true position when measured from the datum. If the nature of the component is such that hole 'B' must be within .005in. from true position relative to hole 'A', then marking both holes from the datum edge and still keeping within the .005in. tolerance band for every measurement would not necessarily give the condition required as hole 'A' could be .005in. nearer the datum edge than the nominal size stated on the drawing, and hole 'B' could be .005in. further from the datum. The situation that now exists, therefore, is that although both holes are within .005in. when measured from the datum, the error between the holes could be .010in. A good, trained, engineering draughtsman will fully understand the nature of the component he is drawing and what duties the component will have to perform and this will affect the way he dimensions the detail drawing. He may have to establish secondary datums, and features relevant to the secondary datum will be dimensioned from this rather than from the main

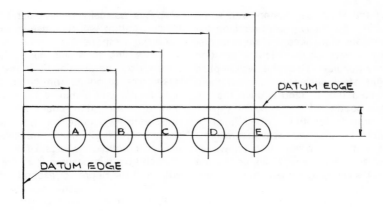

Fig.71a. No secondary datum.

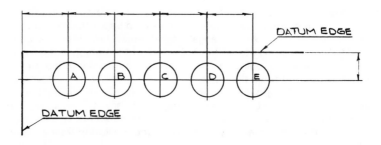

Fig.71b. Holes A,B,C and D are secondary datums

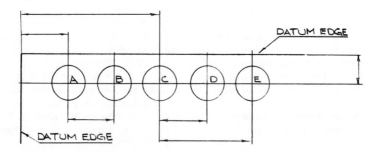

Fig.71c Holes A and C are secondary datums.

datum. Fig.71c shows what appears to be the same pattern of five holes as shown before but the method of dimensioning is different. It now shows that hole 'A' is positioned from the main datum but that hole 'A' has now become the datum for hole 'B'. Hole 'C' is positioned from the main datum but holes 'D' and 'E' are positioned from hole 'C'. In other words, holes 'A' and 'C' have become secondary datums. The five holes no longer form one pattern, they have in fact become two distinct patterns, one pattern being holes 'A' and 'B' centred on 'A', and the other pattern being three holes,'C', 'D' and 'E' centred on hole 'C'.

Another illustration of the establishment of a secondary datum is shown in fig.72. Here we have hole 'A' positioned from the horizontal and vertical datums which are the main datums of the component. The four holes 'B' are positioned from the actual position of hole 'A' and not its true theoretical position fixed by the two ordinates. This means that the four holes marked 'B' will move as a group to follow any error that could arise when establishing the position of the datum hole 'A'. Furthermore, the holes marked 'C' are in turn positioned from the holes marked 'B' and so these 'B' holes are themselves datum holes. It is not usual to get so many datums in one feature but it can happen and this is one of the reasons why it pays to study carefully all the drawings involved in any assembly. For instance, referring back to fig.72, a study of the assembly drawing could reveal that the hole 'A' is in fact a location for a spigoted cover plate similar to the end cover of a steam engine cylinder, with holes 'B' being bolt holes for securing the cover. These securing bolts are prevented from working or vibrating loose by means of a tab washer and the holes 'C' are to accommodate the bent tags of the tab

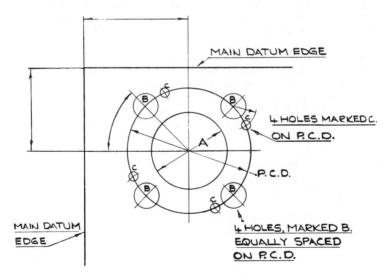

Fig.72 A situation showing two secondary datums. Hole A is located from main datums. Holes B are located from hole A. Holes C are located from holes B.

washers. In industry it would be necessary to manufacture the component and present it as a finished article with all the holes drilled in their correct position. The amateur, in his workshop, will be producing not only the part under consideration but also the cover plate as well and the simplest way for him, therefore, is to drill the bolt holes in the cover plate first and then place the cover in position where it will be located and held by the spigot, and then copy the holes through using the cover plate as a drilling jig. If this method is followed it does not matter if the bolt holes in the cover are out of position, the bolts will still pass through both cover plate and component.

A careful study of the drawings will bring to light all the points similar to those mentioned above and will enable the constructor to plan the method of construction which in turn will indicate how the parts involved should be marked-out.

Most sheet components will be marked-out with the sheet laid down flat on the surface table and using a few of the tools described earlier. A rule, a scriber, a punch, a square and a pair of dividers together with a light hammer are all the tools that are required for marking-out the majority of the components encountered in model making. Most of the lines will be parallel to one of the datum edges and the marking-out process is simply drawing the component as accurately as possible onto the sheet metal. Lines square to a datum edge will naturally be produced by means of the square wherever possible although there may be times when it is not possible to use a square to obtain a perpendicular line. This could arise if the feature is too far away from the datum edge for the square to reach, or if the base line is at an angle to the datum, or it may be that a datum edge is not practical and the marking is being done from a datum line. In these cases the problem of producing a line square to the required datum line can easily be solved by means of elementary geometry. For instance, referring to fig.73a, supposing it is necessary to produce a line perpendicular to the base line A-B. This is done by setting the dividers to a distance somewhat over half the length of the line A-B then, with the dividers, drawing an arc from each of the points A and B. The line C-D, passing through the two intersection points of the arcs, is square to the line A-B and also passes midway between the two points A and B. There could be occasions when the base may be close to an edge of the sheet making this type of construction impractical but it is still possible to construct a right-angle and this construction is shown in fig.73b. In this instance a line is needed perpendicular to line A-B and also passing through point C. The construction is to draw a semi-circle, E-F, centred on C; the actual diameter does not matter but try to get is as large as possible. Then, with the divider legs open as wide as possible, scribe an arc from each of the two points E and F. A line drawn through the intersection of these two arcs and passing through point C will be perpendicular to the line A-B.

There are a great many geometrical constructions that can be made to meet all sorts of conditions and should any reader be interested he will find them in most text books dealing with the subject of geometrical drawing, although very few will be of much value on the amateur's marking-out table.

It is also possible to mark-out sheet metal components with the sheet held vertically but to do this the sheet must be secured to a vertical fixture such as an angle-plate. Naturally, the size of a component that can be held in this manner will depend on the size of the angle-plate

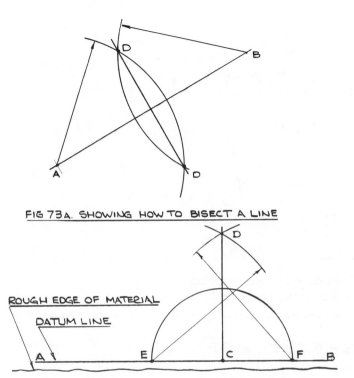

FIG 73A. SHOWING HOW TO BISECT A LINE

Fig.73b. Showing how to constuct a line square to a datum, and passing through a given point.

available. If two angle-plates are to hand then quite long pieces can be successfully held in this way by placing an angle-plate at each end of the component, and it is quite practical to hold workpieces longer than the combined length of the two angle-plates by leaving the centre portion without any backing support. This method of holding permits components such as locomotive frames to be held vertically. The angle-plates need not be a pair as the only feature being used is the vertical face. The photograph, fig.76, shows material mounted this way ready for marking. Securing the sheet to the angle-plates can present a problem. If the plates are the webless type then this will allow clamps such as toolmakers' clamps to be used over the ends but if not then the clamping may have to be done over the top edge of the angle-plate. It may be possible to bolt the sheet onto the angle-plate but this will depend on there being sufficient material available to accommodate the bolt holes without them affecting the finished component.

The advantage of holding sheet vertically is that it is easy to produce longitudinal lines accurately spaced and parallel to each other. When marking with

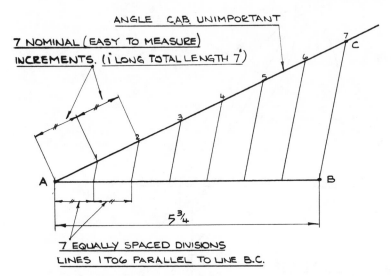

ANGLE C.A.B. UNIMPORTANT

7 NOMINAL (EASY TO MEASURE) INCREMENTS. (1 LONG TOTAL LENGTH 7')

5 3/4

7 EQUALLY SPACED DIVISIONS LINES 1 TO 6 PARALLEL TO LINE B.C.

Fig.74a. Dividing a line into a number of equal parts. The example shows a line 5¾" long divided into 7 parts.

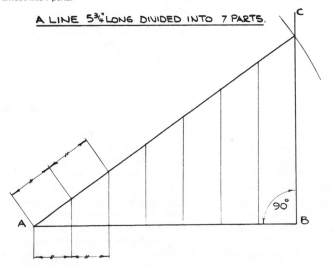

A LINE 5¾" LONG DIVIDED INTO 7 PARTS.

90°

Fig.74b. A modified construction to the above. Line B.C. is now square to the base line. Point C is determined by scribing an arc length AC from point A.

the sheet laid flat on the table, a longitudinal line is produced by measuring and making a mark at the required distance from the datum at both ends of the required line and then joining the marks by means of a straight edge. This allows for three chances of making an error and not obtaining a line parallel to the datum. However, when the workpiece is held vertically these long lines can be made with a scribing block, surface gauge or height vernier and all lines marked this way will be parallel to each other and to the datum, always assuming that the datum has been placed into contact with the surface plate, or on a pair of parallel strips. Vertical lines can be more troublesome as it may not always be possible to get the blade of the square into contact with the face of the sheet owing to the stock of the square being of thicker material than the blade.

As both vertical and horizontal attitudes of holding the workpieces possess certain advantages then both may be used in the marking-out of a component. If it is a relatively long component then all longitudinal lines can be scribed on with the material secured to a pair of angle-plates; the sheet can then be placed down flat onto the marking-table for all the other features to be outlined.

Another construction that the author has found useful is that of dividing a line into a number of equal parts. This can, of course, be done by stepping out on a trial and error basis with a pair of dividers but a more scientific way is shown in fig.74a. Supposing it is required to divide the line A-B into seven equal parts and that the length of the line is $5\frac{1}{4}$in. Doing this mathematically would produce an increment length of 23/28in. This is not a particularly 'nice' size to measure but fortunately there is no need to do this. Start by drawing the line A-C, the angle between this and the base line is unimpor-

tant as the construction will work with any angle although about 30° is most satisfactory. Choosing any convenient size, mark out seven divisions along this line. For the purpose of this exercise it will be convenient to make each division one inch long but, again, it does not matter what particular increment is chosen so long as all seven are the same. Next, join the last point C with point B on the base line thus completing a triangle, then all that remains to be done is to draw lines parallel to line C-B passing through all the incremental points. The point where these lines intersect the base line indicates the position of the divisions required. This type of construction requires the use of a tool such as the protractor or combination set in order to draw the parallel angled lines. However, if all that is available is the square then the above method can be modified as shown in fig.74b. Here, a line is drawn from point B perpendicular to the base line. Decide what increment to use and multiply this by the number of increments and this will give you the length of the line A-C. Since, in this case, the increment is one-inch and the number of increments required is seven, the length of the line A-C will be seven inches. With the dividers or trammels set at this size and with one point on position A, mark the intersection point on the perpendicular line thus determining the position of C. All that now remains is to mark the remaining six points on the line A-C then drop perpendicular lines onto the base line by means of the try-square.

One thing that all designers try to avoid is sharp corners. All corners wherever possible should have a blending radius between the two meeting faces. In sheet metal components this radius is usually formed by drilling holes at all the required places before any general cutting is undertaken. This means that the centres of the holes must be marked onto the sheet. With right-angle corners this is simple and is shown in fig.75a. The centre of the radius is found by producing the square in the corner, the length of the side being the size of the radius required. If a line A-D is drawn through the centre of the radius it will be seen that this line bisects the angle between the two sides. In this case, as the angle is 90°, then the angle of the line A-D is at 45° to either of the two datum edges. There will be cases where the hole centre will need locating and the angle between the two respective sides not necessarily 90°. As was seen above with the right-angle, the hole centre lay along a line that bisected the two sides and this applies to any angle, therefore, if the angle between the two sides is bisected it will give a line which passes through the hole centre. It does not matter if the angle is less, or more, than 90°, the method will still be the same and as illustrated in fig.75b. With the dividers set at a convenient size, scribe an arc from the centre A cutting the two sides and determining points B and C, then, again with the dividers and using points B and C, scribe arcs to determine the intersection point D. A line drawn from point A passing through point D will bisect the angle and give a line upon which the hole centre must rest. The actual position can be found by setting the dividers to the radius required and with one point on the scribed line move the divider along the line until a point is reached that allows the radius to blend smoothly into the two sides. Alter-

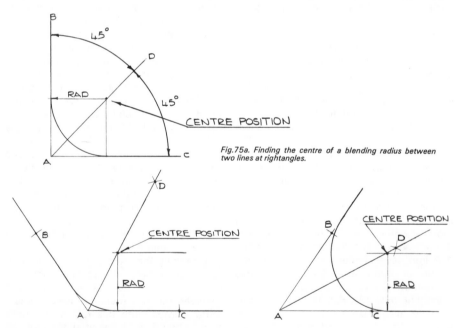

Fig.75a. Finding the centre of a blending radius between two lines at rightangles.

Fig. 75b. Showing how to find the centre of a blending radius between two lines not at right angles.

94

Fig.76 This shows a sheet component — such as a locomotive frame — secured to two angle-plates for marking out. It is much easier to obtain horizontal parallel lines by using this method. The larger of the angle-plates is a webbed pattern. This presents problems in clamping; as can be seen a toolmaker's clamp has been used with one screw passing through one of the slots in the angle-plate.

natively, the position can be constructed, again referring to fig.75b, by drawing a line parallel to either the line A-B or A-C but at a distance away equal to the radius required and where this line meets the line A-D will be the position of the centre required.

MARKING-OUT CASTINGS

All the comments made above about drawings, and the interpretation of drawings made with regard to sheet metal parts, also apply when dealing with the marking-out and manufacture of components produced from castings, forgings or bar stock material. There is, however, one big difference between the drawing showing a component made from sheet material and the drawing showing 'solid' or three-dimensional components. All the information for a sheet component, other than the thickness of the sheet, can usually be given on one view, but with other components this is not so and it may be necessary to show quite a number of views. A simple cube, for instance, has six faces and if only one hole is required in each face it may be necessary to show six views of the one cube. Hidden features which cannot be seen on the face of any view may appear as dotted lines and this method of depicting 'out of sight' features is satisfactory if the component is relatively simple, but if the component is complex with a number of hidden features such as holes, counter bores, pockets, etc., then the number of dotted lines can be confusing. It is also poor drawing practice to give dimensions to dotted lines as this only adds to the confusion. It is the draughtsman's duty to remove confusion because if a drawing can be misread it will almost certainly be misread — in fact some craftsmen take a delight in doing so! In order, therefore, to avoid the use of dotted lines, sections are taken and shown on the drawing. A section is a view showing what would be seen if the component were to be cut at the section line. Sections are easily recognised because it is general practice to show all material cut by the section 'cross-hatched' which means that lines, usually at 45°, are shown covering the whole of the area cut by the section. It follows from the above that there can be quite a number of views required in order to give all the information needed to mark-out and machine a casting. These views are not just drawn anywhere on the drawing sheet but follow a set pattern and it helps if the constructor is familiar with this pattern. Mistaking one view for some other can lead to incorrect interpretation of the drawing.

It is unfortunate but there are two patterns or systems that can be used by the draughtsman when setting out a detail drawing. For the correct interpretation of the drawing it is necessary for the reader of that drawing to be familiar with both systems and to be able to recognise which system has been used on the drawing he is studying. The two systems are known as 'First Angle projection' and 'Third Angle projection', sometimes called English projection and American projection respectively. For many years all drawings

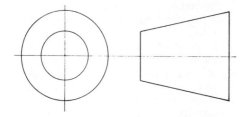

Fig.77a The universally accepted diagram denoting third angle projection. This diagram usually appears on all third angle drawings.

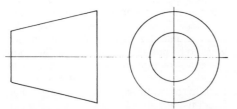

Fig.77b. How the above diagram would appear if drawn in first angle. Note – this is shown for demonstration purposes only. This diagram should never appear on first angle projection drawings.

produced in the U.K. were drawn in first angle, however, a change has now been made and almost all commercial engineering drawings are produced third angle, with the result that this method is now becoming universally accepted as standard practice. Model engineers seem to always be the last people to change and accept new practices and their drawings are no exception. Most of the drawings available, and some still being made, are in first angle projection and almost all the 'works' drawings or prototypes such as traction engines, locomotives, marine and stationary engines that are available to modellers were made generally over 50 years ago and as such will be first angle projection. This is neither the place nor the time to discuss the merits of one system over another but it is necessary to show what the differences are and how to recognise them.

First angle drawings rarely carry any notation stating that the drawing is first angle but almost all commercial third angle drawings do carry a note stating 'Third Angle projection'. In fact there is a universally accepted diagram (logo) which appears somewhere around the border of the drawing, or in the title block, which illustrates that the drawing is in third angle projection. Fig.77 shows this diagram although on the drawing sheet it will be produced to a very small scale, the whole thing being only about half-an-inch long. What the diagram represents is a frustum of a cone together with an end view. It is the position of the end view showing the two concentric circles that indicates the method of projection being used. The side view of the cone frustum does not indicate that it is a cone, it is the end view that does this. If the cone were viewed from the large end then only one circle would be seen as the other end, being smaller, would be hidden; but if the cone were viewed from the small end then not only would this small end be seen but the larger end also would be visible, even though it is behind the small end. The first view would, therefore, be one large circle while the second view would be two circles. This end view can be placed at either end of the side view and so, referring to fig.77, it would be possible for this end view showing the two concentric circles to be placed on the right hand of the side view instead of being on the left hand side as shown. This position would indicate first angle projection, see fig.77b. The difference between third angle and first angle projection is that in third angle projection drawings the view is shown on the side being looked at whilst in first angle drawings the view is shown on the opposite side to that being viewed. This principle is applied to all views and sections shown on the drawing and is illustrated in fig.78 where two tapered holes at right angles to one another are shown in a cube – drawing A being third angle projection while drawing B is first angle.

Many times it will not matter if the projection is not recognised but there are times when failure to understand the projection could lead to machining the component incorrectly. This is best illustrated by referring to fig.79. Here we see a component where the shape is similar viewed from either end. If the drawing were third angle, then the three small holes would be positioned in the same end as the flange with the group of four holes in the opposite end, but if the projection were first angle then the relative positions would be reversed and the four hole group would be in the same end as the flange with the three hole group in the end away from the flange. As this illustrates, it pays to study the drawing carefully and fully understand

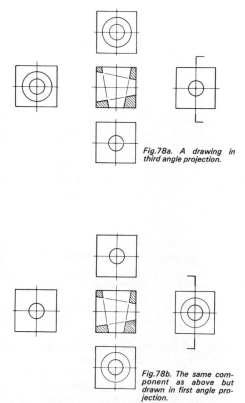

Fig.78a. A drawing in third angle projection.

Fig.78b. The same component as above but drawn in first angle projection.

the drawing requirements before any attempt is made to start production on what could be a costly casting.

When castings are received from the foundry they are very rough, have sharp edges and contain sand and scale in the 'skin'. Before any marking or machining is undertaken it is a good idea to give them a good fettle, which not only makes them more pleasant to handle but also removes the hard and unwanted particles that are deleterious to both the machine and the tools used on them. Some people suggest soaking or pickling iron castings in a weak

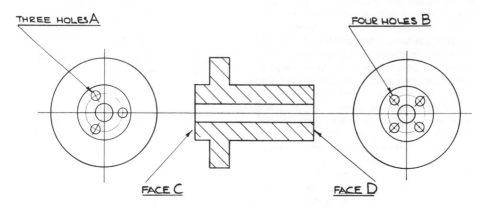

Fig.79 With the drawing shown above it is vital to know what projection has been used.

The small diagram denotes third angle projection, so the holes A are in face C, and the holes B are in face D.

If the drawing is read as first angle projection, then the holes A would be incorrectly drilled in face D, and holes B incorrectly drilled in face C.

solution of either sulphuric or hydrochloric acid, and treating bronze castings in a similar way with weak nitric acid. Although this will clean the castings nicely the author prefers to attack all castings with a few old files. Do not use new files on unmachined castings otherwise they will not be in the 'new' condition very long! It is a good idea when an old file is replaced with a new one to keep the old file for fettling purposes rather than throwing it away. After all the roughness has been removed the casting can be given a coat of white emulsion paint as this helps to give a good contrasting surface for the marking-out.

With castings or other components made from stock material, the initial measuring work will be to 'prove' the casting or material. This means to make sure that the material or casting is large enough in all aspects to allow the component to be produced to the drawing requirements. A point to keep in mind when marking-out and machining a casting is to not remove too much material from any one face as this may adversely affect some other feature. An allowance for machining will have been made where machining is required but this allowance may not be constant for all surfaces and removing too much from one feature may mean that there is an insufficient machining allowance elsewhere. Deciding how much material to remove from a feature, particularly a datum face, is a part of the proving process.

Unlike sheet metal components, it is not practical to complete all the marking-out on a casting before machining commences. There is little point in marking-out the rough face on a casting if that same face has to be machined as the machining process will remove all the marks that have been made on it. The method must be to mark what is practical then perform the machining operations relative to those marks and then return

98

the component to the marking-out table for the next stage. It is a case of producing the component stage-by-stage.

The first, and an important, decision is to fix the main datum both for marking and machining. The drawing should be a help here by noting what the draughtsman has chosen for the dimensioning datum and, if possible, using the same feature. If the drawing datum is a flat face then producing this face should be the first machining operation as this will make the ideal datum for all subsequent marking and machining operations. A typical example here would be a locomotive slide valve cylinder where the flat datum face would be the bolting face or the valve face. On some locomotive cylinders, particularly the piston valve type, the drawing datum may be the centre line of the main bore and if this is so then the valve bore will be dimensioned from the main bore and not from the bolting face. In circumstances like this it may be advantageous from the production point of view to make the bolting face the datum and produce both bores from this face. There will be some components where the main datum will be the centre line of a bore or hole, there being no machined face called for on the drawing. This is perfectly acceptable drawing practice but it can present the constructor with a problem as the centre line of a hole is only a line or point in space and is not a tangible feature from which to make a measurement. In cases like this it may be necessary to set up a marking and machining datum. This service datum, as it is called, may serve no useful purpose once the component is finished, but to produce the component without it would be exceedingly difficult. A good model designer may foresee a problem of this type and call for a service datum to be incorporated into the casting and also to show it on the drawing. In this case the drawing will suggest that this feature is removed from the component after all the machining operations have been carried out. On some occasions the author has brazed a piece onto a casting to act as a service lug or datum, this, of course, being removed after it has served its purpose.

The marking-out of castings will in the main be carried out on the surface plate using the surface gauge to produce all lines parallel to the base or chosen datum. It may be necessary to bolt the component onto an angle-plate for the marking-out. If so, then this angle-plate can also be stood on its end, thus effectively moving the component through 90° and providing a ready-made datum for producing lines at right-angles. It may be that the component can be left firmly secured to the angle-plate for the machining operation and this could be a decided advantage as the angle-plate can be easily fastened onto the lathe faceplate or boring table cross-slide or any other machine table. This will considerably ease any setting-up problems that could otherwise arise because the marked lines will automatically be either parallel or square to the machine table.

Where castings are concerned the model engineer will find that very little marking-out on the surface plate will be needed, particularly if the method of machining is carefully studied and planned. Much of the measuring required can be done on and by the actual machine tool being used.

Machining operations required on castings consist mainly of boring holes and producing faces square to them, machining flat surfaces to provide a surface for bolting onto some mating part, and drilling and tapping holes for screws and studs. Much of this work can be performed without any prior marking-out as machine tool tables are moved by means of screws and nuts and these provide the basis of an accurate means of measuring. It was described earlier how the micrometer is basically a screw and nut and although the feed screws of general purpose machine tools are not produced to the same high degree of accuracy with regard to pitch errors as are micrometer screws, they are nevertheless very accurate and can be used as a basis for measurement. It is common practice on small imperial machine tools to fit 10-threads-per-inch feed screws on all slideways, the pitch, therefore, is .100in. These screws are also usually fitted with a friction driven micrometer or index dial and these dials are marked into 100 divisions, thus moving the dial one division moves the sliding table and the workpiece .001in.

The lathe has provision for moving the tool in two planes, up and down the bed by means of the leadscrew or top slide, and at right angles to the bed by means of the cross-slide. On lathes produced for the amateur, such as the Myford range, the cross-slide itself is provided with tee-slots and is known as a boring table cross-slide. If the top slide is removed the boring table provides a flat true surface on which workpieces can be readily secured. Castings should not, of course, be bolted directly onto the boring table as this may mark or even indent the surface. If a piece of thin card is placed between the casting and the table not only will the table be protected but also a firmer hold will be obtained. The workpiece can now be moved in two planes and under the control of the micrometer dials. It must be pointed out, however, that the handwheel on the end of the leadscrew of most imperial lathes will have 125 divisions as it is general practice to use 8-tpi leadscrews. This makes no difference to the method being discussed but it is important to remember that one turn of the handwheel does not give the same displacement as one turn of the cross-slide screw.

There is now a means of accurately controlling the movement of the workpiece, in fact what has been done is to transform the lathe into a two-axis jig borer. In industrial toolrooms, holes that have to be accurately spaced are not produced by marking-out and then drilling to the marks, but by means of jig borers. These are machine tools somewhat similar to a vertical milling machine but are built to a very high standard of accuracy. Workpieces clamped to these machines can be moved within very fine limits of size, so fine in fact that these machines are kept in specially temperature-controlled rooms in order to avoid any problems that would arise due to thermal expansion! Our improvised jig borer, although not in the same professional class, is nevertheless capable of producing work to a high degree of accuracy, far greater than could be achieved by the normal process of marking-out, and this method of measuring on the machine itself is to be recommended and should be used wherever it is practical to do so.

When using the lathe as a borer the relative positions of the tool and the workpiece are reversed. The tool is secured into a suitable holder which in turn is fastened onto the lathe mandrel, and instead of the workpiece revolving and the tool being clamped as in normal lathework, the workpiece is clamped and the tool revolves. The type of tool used will depend on the nature of the work being performed. For general facing duties a fly-cutter with only a small overhang will give excellent results. For general boring work the tool can be held in a bar between centres or, in the case of blind holes, on an overhanging bar. A boring head vastly increases the scope of the machine and is an accessory well worth acquiring. Commercial boring heads tend to be expensive but home-made ones are just as useful and they are not difficult to make. Ordinary drilled holes can be produced by holding the drill in the normal drill chuck which is secured in the Morse taper of the lathe mandrel.

If all the holes are on the same straight line and the workpiece is secured to the lathe cross-slide with this line coincidental with the lathe axis, then any desired point on the line can be positioned and repeated by means of the cross-slide handwheel. The depth of any feature can also be accurately measured by using the handwheel on the end of the leadscrew. Care must always be taken to eliminate the back-lash that will be present in the feedscrew and nuts and this is done by moving the relative slide in the same direction when it is being used to obtain a setting. It is also a help if the micrometer dials are zeroed on the datum as this eliminates, or simplifies, any calculation that may be needed to achieve the desired setting.

There is one big drawback in the arrangement outlined above and that is the lack of a third axis. Where height variations are necessary some means must be found for providing this facility. If the variations in height require only one movement of the workpiece, such as would be needed to produce the two bores of a locomotive piston valve cylinder, then this can be accomplished by means of a packing strip. This packing strip will have to be made to a thickness equal to the distance between the two bores measured in the relative plane. The machining sequence will be to set the cylinder casting bolting face down on the lathe cross-slide with sufficient packing under it to bring the centre line of the main bore coincident with the lathe axis. The main bore can then be machined with a boring bar mounted between centres or by means of a boring head. The end face of the casting nearest to the headstock should also be machined at this setting and the casting will then have to be removed from the cross-slide and the packing strip inserted between the cross-slide and the cylinder casting. This will now bring the piston valve bore onto the plane of the lathe centre. In order to assist in re-setting the casting square with the lathe axis, use can be made of the machined end face. Setting this parallel to the lathe face-plate will automatically set the main bore square again. The piston valve bore can now be produced following the same procedure as used when producing the main bore. It could be that the valve bore of the cylinder casting may be above the main bore when the casting is resting on the cross-slide, if this is so then the special packing would be inserted to obtain the main bore setting and removed for the valve bore setting. The details are unimportant here, it is the principle of the removable packing that is being illustrated.

Unfortunately it does mean that every time a height adjustment is required, the workpiece will have to be removed from the machine, a packing of the correct thickness inserted and the workpiece then reset to its original position relative to the lathe axis. Sometimes this can be a relatively simple matter but generally speaking the removal of the workpiece and its relocation between machining operations is undesirable. It is in these cases that it becomes necessary to introduce a controllable third axis and this can be a vertical slide. This slide is secured on the lathe cross-slide with the workpiece then fastened onto the vertical face of the slide and there is now a vertical controllable movement available which can be used in a similar manner to the cross-slide. Another advantage of the vertical slide is that they often have the facility of being able to swivel in two planes, thus further increasing the versatility of the machine. There are, naturally, disadvantages in using a vertical slide and one of them is that by introducing another slideway into the machine some loss of rigidity must be expected. Another, and one that the author finds particularly annoying, is that because the workpiece is mounted vertically it is necessary for the operator to bend over sideways in order to have a clear view of both the setting and machining operations. At night working on the vertical slide can, literally, be a pain in the neck! However, this is a small price to pay for the added versatility gained.

It was stated above that the tool room jig borer is similar in principle to the vertical milling machine and constructors who possess, or have access to, a vertical miller can use it with great advantage as a jig borer. The vertical miller is a very useful general purpose machine tool and is only second to the lathe in its versatility. If full use is made of the vertical milling machine then a great deal of marking-out on both castings and platework can be eliminated. The milling machine is much more rigid than the lathe for this type of work and as the workpiece is secured in a horizontal attitude, operators have an excellent view of both the setting and machine operations. When a workpiece is clamped onto the table of a vertical milling machine it is under the influence of both table and cross-slide feedscrews and it therefore follows that by using the micrometer dials fitted to these screws, the workpiece can be moved any specific amount in two planes. If all the holes required in any group are related to a datum hole then it is a simple matter to zero both micrometer dials on this datum. The feedscrews can then be used in order to obtain the desired position of any new feature, and the workpiece can then easily be restored to the original zero setting of the datum ready for positioning the next hole. If one of the holes required is large and is best produced by boring, a boring head screwed onto the mandrel nose of the machine will enable any size of hole to be accurately produced. It does not matter if, between drilling holes, the drill chuck is removed and replaced by a milling cutter in order to produce new surfaces: so long as the workpiece is not removed from the machine and the micrometer dials are not interfered with, the original datum setting can always be achieved. It is therefore possible to perform a considerable amount of accurate work on the vertical miller without any actual marking-out other than that required to determine the position of the original datum.

Frequently, holes are shown on drawings as being placed around a bore and on a pitch circle diameter. A typical example of this type of arrangement is where the holes are required to secure a cylinder cover plate onto the cylinder block. The method just outlined does not permit any means of rotating the workpiece about a centre so in order to produce holes around a pitch circle diameter it will be necessary to transpose the method of dimensioning the holes from an angular

Fig.80 Producing holes on a pitch circle diameter. The chuck and workpiece have been removed from the lathe and placed on a special rotary device secured to the table of a vertical milling machine. Any P.C.D. can be obtained by controlling movement of the milling table and any angle obtained by means of the micrometer dial on the rotary device. A drilling machine could be used instead of a milling machine but the off-set to obtain the required P.C.D. would have to be obtained by measurement.

position around a circle and place them on ordinates, then the relative movement can be given by the two feedscrews. This method is perfectly satisfactory although it does call for some simple calculations to be made.

In the majority of cases it will not be necessary to produce the holes at this stage. For instance, in the case mentioned above the holes in the cylinder block will be positioned by placing the corresponding cover on the block and copying the holes through the cover. The holes in the cover will naturally have to be positioned but again there is a simple method of achieving this without the need of marking-out each hole individually, in fact, the holes can be drilled in the correct position after the completion of the turning operations on the cover but while it is still held in the lathe chuck. What is required is a means of being able to hold the workpiece – still in the chuck – under the drill with the facility to be able to rotate it a controlled amount about its own axis.

This can be accomplished by the use of

a rotary table and an adaptor. Most rotary tables have a tee-slotted table top or plate on which workpieces can be bolted, and usually, these also have a hole in the centre of the table. A fixture or mandrel can be produced which will locate in this central hole and if the nose of this mandrel is provided with the same screw and register configuration as that of the lathe then this will permit the lathe chuck to be mounted onto the rotary table. The mandrel can be secured to the rotary table by bolting through a flange and into the tee-slots.

This rotary table can then be positioned on the table of the vertical milling machine so that the centre of the table and the spindle of the milling machine are coincident. The miller table can then be moved an amount equal to a half of the P.C.D. required; the micrometer dial on the feedscrew will give this displacement to a degree of accuracy far greater than could be expected to be achieved with a rule. Both the table and cross-slide of the milling machine are then locked into position. The chuck, still

103

holding the cylinder cover, can then be removed from the lathe and placed on the rotary table, the rotary table index collar set at zero and the first hole drilled. The rotary table can now be used as a dividing head to obtain the correct amount of angular movement. For instance, if ten equally spaced holes are required and the driving gear on the rotary table has 60-teeth then every six complete turns of the handwheel will give the displacement required; if the rotary table has 90-teeth then nine turns of the handle will be required, and so on. The result will be ten holes equally spaced with a high degree of accuracy and with no marking or measuring done to produce them, see fig.80.

It could be interpreted from the above comments that marking-out is superfluous and that all that has been said earlier about marking-out, and the tools to use, may be interesting but of little practical value. This, of course, is not true; all the tools discussed have practical uses and important roles to play in the workshop, although few workshops will possess all of them. The point being made is that before commencing construction of any component, carefully plan the method to be used. The actual path followed will naturally depend on the equipment available, and the fact that newly-acquired tools are to hand does not mean that they should be used if the component under construction can be made more easily, quickly and accurately by some other means.

It is not possible to give instructions on the way any one component should be made as this again depends not only on the component but also on the experience of the constructor and the tools he has at his disposal. Many wonderful pieces of work have come out of very sparsely equipped workshops, illustrating that the most important factor is not the tools but how they are used. Expertise cannot be taught, it has to be acquired by practical experience. What can be done, and what I hope this book is doing, is to point the way. If tools are used in a manner that experience gained by others has shown to give the best results, then the amateur is following good practice and will get more satisfaction out of his efforts.

Much of what has been said during this chapter has dealt not so much with marking-out but with the use of machine tools. Although the two are often inseparable, machine tools and their uses is really another subject and so it has not been fully covered in detail. What has been done is to bring to the notice of the reader the fact that machine tools are capable of doing more than merely producing swarf, they can in themselves be measuring devices and, indeed, may well be the most accurate means of measuring that the workshop possesses.

CHAPTER 10

A Summary involving a practical example

It has been stated in this book on more than one occasion that the method of manufacture and assembly used in the amateur or model engineering workshop can be totally different from the method used in modern industry. This is reflected in the way things are measured and the degree of accuracy needed to complete a successful assembly. An example was given in chapter 1 of a piston and cylinder and how, if one is made to fit the other with the correct amount of working clearances between the two parts, the nominal size is of little importance since a limited deviation on either side of nominal will not have any effect on the working of the complete cylinder assembly. This is a simple and obvious example but there are many others neither simple nor obvious and the author considered that as a concluding chapter he would choose a more complex example and follow it through step-by-step, which would not only emphasise the point being made but would also be of practical use to some constructors. Most model engineers, at some time or another in their modelling careers, produce a small steam locomotive, so an example relating to the construction of some items on this type of model has been chosen.

Experience has shown that the problem that causes most concern to the tyro, and sometimes to the more experienced craftsman as well, is that of obtaining a smooth working fit of the coupling rods. All too often it is obvious, when examining models at exhibitions, that the constructor has had difficulties in getting the rods and wheels to rotate freely and has 'solved' the problem by producing the coupling rod bushes at both ends of the rod with excessive working clearance. It is true that the locomotive engine is not a fixed geometry engine and that some clearance is necessary in the coupling rod bushes to allow the wheels to move up and down under the influence of the springs. However, when this clearance, required to allow for small vertical movement of the axle boxes, is additional to the clearance necessary to obtain free movement with the wheels in normal running position, the final result can often be decidedly sloppy rods.

The author was fully aware of the problems that were involved when he started to make his first locomotive. This was many years ago whilst he was still a student apprentice and very proud of his newly acquired skill of being able to work to fine limits. The result was that care was taken in producing all the parts to as near nominal size as possible and occasionally borrowing measuring equipment in order to satisfy himself that everything was being made to the highest degree of accuracy that he could attain. The final result, which took a considerable amount of time to achieve, was reasonable, but even so some clearance had to be given to the coupling rod bushes in order to get smooth rotation of the wheels and rods. Since those days he has had time to sit and think and although all the precision involved was a good exercise, it was not really necessary. He would build the same unit to-day with possibly better results but using no measuring tool other than an engineer's steel rule. Whilst the end results may well be the same, the methods used in the production of the component parts would be totally different, the differences arising from the fact that the unit would be looked upon as a whole rather than as a collection of pieces.

When faced with any problem the first and most important step in seeking a solution is to fully understand the problem. An examination of the coupling rod problem shows that there are many parts involved in the assembly and that a dimensional error in any one adversely affects the fit of the coupling rods. Only a small error in each of a number of components adds up to a considerable error in the final assembly. It is no use hoping that the errors will cancel each other out — nature does not work that way! Firstly, then, let us consider the problem as a collection of parts and then try to produce each component as accurately to the drawing size as possible. This method of building is frequently followed by constructors, the general idea being to make a component to the drawing and then put it in a box and start another and so on un-til eventually enough parts have been made to commence assembly. Following this method, the frames would be carefully marked-out and then cut and filed to shape. The feature on the frames that influences the problem under discussion is the rectangular slots that locate the horn blocks, the centre distance between these slots being, naturally, the same as the hole centre distance of the coupling rods. By marking, measuring and filing, or machining with extreme care, the average constructor would do very well to get the slots positioned to within .003in. of true position. Even with limits as close as this the total error between the two slots could be .006in. either side of datum.

The horn blocks that fit into the slots would now be machined, and to maintain the correct nominal distance between the axle centres these horn blocks must be symmetrical about their centre lines. If this centre line is only .001in. out of true position this will add a further .002in. error either side of datum, making a total of .008in. either side. The axle boxes must also be made symmetrical about their centre line and assuming that the hole for the axle is only .001in. out of position then this will add a further .002in. to the grand total. Other factors that also affect the final result are the concentricity of the axles and wheel seats and also the concentricity of the coupling rod bushes, although, if these turned items are correctly produced and the reaming size for the bushes is obtained by boring rather than by drilling, we can discount the effect of any error introduced by these turned items. It can now be seen why the beginner to model engineering gets into trouble with coupling rods. Even by working to close limits it may be necessary to give .020in. clearance in the rod bushes in order to get the wheels to turn. Many constructors would find it difficult to work to limits as close as those mentioned in the above example and as a consequence the remedy would be 'sloppy rods'.

If, before any construction was commenced, the problem was carefully thought out, it would be realised that all that is required is to produce the coupling rods in such as way as to ensure that the centre distance between the two crank pin holes in the rods is the same as, or as near as possible the same as, the distance between the two axle centres. One way of achieving this is to assemble the frames, horn blocks, axle box and axles, etc., and then accurately measure the actual distance between the two axle centres. With this size known the problem is now reduced to producing only the coupling rod centres to a high degree of accuracy. This, however, would not be easy to accomplish without the necessary measuring tools required to span the rod centres and few workshops are likely to have measuring equipment large enough to achieve this.

On the other hand, the whole problem can be examined from a different viewpoint – it can be turned round! Supposing the coupling rods were made first and the axle centre distance made to suit the rods. The end result would be just as satisfactory as trying to produce the rods to match the axles, so let us examine the possibility of achieving this. The rods can be made and the centre distance produced by measuring with an engineer's steel rule. Marked-out and made in this way would produce rods with possibly a linear error of .005in. or even .010in. between the crank pin holes, but this will not matter if the axle centres are made to suit – even the scale enthusiast who likes everything 'just so' would not notice if the axle centres were .010in. wider or narrower than 'scale'.

The rods can be completed and even have the bushes fitted although with the smaller engines it may be better not to fit the bushes as this will reduce the size of the bore and make subsequent operations a little tricky. Naturally, the rods must be made as a pair and clamped together for boring-out the crank pin holes. If this were not done then it would be possible to get one side of the engine longer than the other!

The rods can now be laid aside and a start made on the frames. The slots for the horn blocks can be marked-out using a steel rule since no greater accuracy need be strived for than can be obtained by the rule. The slots themselves are produced in the normal way of cutting and filing to the lines. The horn blocks are machined to fit the slots in the frames and, again, the actual exact width of the slots and horn blocks is not important as it is the fit between the two components that matters. This fit should not be sloppy otherwise it will be the rivets securing the hornblocks to the frames that will have to take the thrust produced by the cylinders and this is not a desirable state of affairs as it would quickly lead to the horn blocks working loose. The horn blocks can be fitted to the frames individually, concentrating on obtaining the correct fit in the frames rather than worrying about what is happening to the nominal centre distance.

The next components to consider are the axle boxes and it is these items, or at least the holes through them, that actually locate the position of the axles. Any discrepancy from nominal dimensions that has arisen in producing all the other parts can be compensated for if the holes are bored, not necessarily in the centre of each axle box as the drawing will show, but in such a position as to bring the axle centres back into their desired position.

The actual dimension required is not the nominal size between the axles but the actual centre distance of the coupling rod holes. The whole problem is therefore solved by boring the axle boxes to suit the coupling rods previously made. This is not a difficult task and can easily be done without the need of any measuring equipment at all. The total error involved will not be large, probably no more than about 1/32in. The size of the axle boxes will be such as to allow the bore for the axle to be moved by this amount without affecting any other feature. This being so, one pair of axle boxes for one axle can be produced in the normal way and all the compensation needed can be obtained on the other pair of boxes.

Therefore, make, fit and finish one pair of axle boxes and then place them in their respective horn blocks and clamp them in the correct running position. The other pair can be finished in every respect except for the axle bore which needs to be made much smaller than the finished size, say about $\frac{1}{4}$in. for a $\frac{1}{2}$in. diameter axle. One of these axle boxes should also be clamped in the correct running position. It is important to clamp the axle boxes in position and not fit them on their springs because in order to obtain best results both axle boxes must be rigid with the frame assembly. Next produce a dummy axle for the first pair of boxes, this being simply a straight piece of steel bar that will just slide nicely into the two bearing holes, then turn down one end of the dummy axle to a sliding fit into the hole in the end of the coupling rod. While it does not really matter which end of the rod fits onto the dummy axle it may be as well to choose the end that will eventually fit the crank pin of the wheel that fits onto that particular axle. A bush is now required to fit into the hole in the other end of the coupling rod – any material will do for the

bush as it is only a 'service' component; mild steel will be perfectly satisfactory. This bush should also be a nice sliding fit into the rod end, but it must also be slightly longer than the width of the rod end so that it will protrude slightly beyond the face of the rod. The bush should be hollow with a hole through the centre about 3/16th in. or so in diameter. Now select a screw or bolt that will pass through this hole (2BA will do) and is also long enough to pass through the axle box. The head of the screw must be smaller than the outside diameter of the bush to ensure that the bush and screw will both pass completely through the hole in the coupling rod end.

The coupling rod is now placed into position on the 'chassis', one end onto the dummy axle. Place the bush into the other end of the rod and swing the rod into position so that the screw will pass through both bush and axle box and then put a washer and nut onto the end of the screw. Position the rod so that it is parallel to the centre line of the axles and then tighten the screw. This will clamp the bush onto the 'small hole' axle box, see fig.81. The coupling rod can then be removed. We now know that the centre distance between the axis of the axle and axis of the bush is similar to the length between the coupling rod holes. The axle box screw assembly is then removed from the frames and set up in the four-jaw chuck until the bush runs truly. The bolt is then loosened and the nut and button removed, the hole in the axle box can then be bored to the finished size. When the axle box is replaced in the frame the axle centres will be similar to the coupling rod centres. The whole process can then be repeated for the other side of the engine.

The only remaining work that influences the free working of the coupling

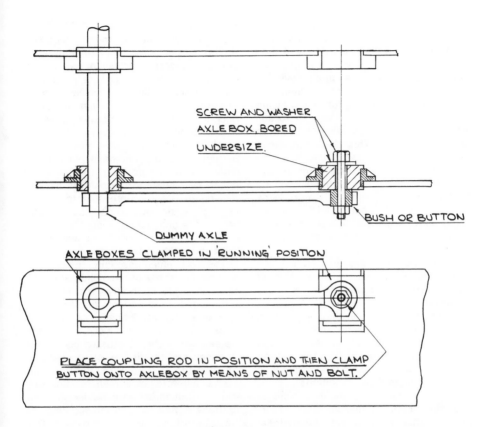

SCREW AND WASHER

AXLE BOX, BORED

UNDERSIZE.

BUSH OR BUTTON

DUMMY AXLE

AXLE BOXES CLAMPED IN 'RUNNING' POSITION

PLACE COUPLING ROD IN POSITION AND THEN CLAMP
BUTTON ONTO AXLEBOX BY MEANS OF NUT AND BOLT.

Fig.81 Showing how to obtain correctly fitted coupling rods without the need for direct accurate measurement.

rods is the boring of the crank pin holes and the fitting of the crank pins. The method chosen for boring the holes must ensure that all the crank pins have the same throw. The well-known method of clamping the wheels to an eccentrically mounted fixture on the lathe faceplate is recommended as this will not only guarantee that all the crank throws are similar but will also ensure that the holes are square to the face of the wheels. This is not the place to describe this method in full as it is basically a machining rather than a measuring exercise but if any reader is in doubt it is recommended that he reads about it in a book dealing specially with the problems encountered in machining.

For the sake of simplicity, only the coupling of two axles has been described as the point being made is to outline the basic principle involved. The same principle can, naturally, be employed when building engines with three or more sets of wheels.

One of the main themes of this book has been that in the amateur's workshop a high degree of linear accuracy is not usually necessary as a small deviation from the nominal size of a component can usually be compensated for by producing its mating part in such a way as to still arrive at the desired working fit between two components. This does not mean that careless or poor work can be easily rectified, or that the constructor can go blundering on assuming that all will be right in the end. Should this attitude be adopted then all most certainly will not come right in the end, in fact, the 'end' will probably be an empty workbench and a full scrap bin.

Before commencing any project the prospective builder should make himself familiar with all the parts that are finally assembled together. Find out where they all fit and what function they all perform, then decide what is vital to achieve the desired end product and what is of less importance. Then he can plan the method of construction and measuring techniques required to meet these conditions.

As we have seen, some latitude is allowable in linear dimensions but, unfortunately, this is not so with geometrical deviations. A geometrical error once made cannot usually be rectified by making its mating part in such a way as to compensate for the error originally made. This most important subject of geometrics is outside the scope of "Measuring and Marking" because geometrical accuracy is not obtained by measuring but by choosing the correct machining techniques to suit any par-ticular problem encountered. This is a most important subject and one that cannot be over-emphasised as the difference between success and failure can simply rest on choosing the correct machining programme. To illustrate the importance of geometrics it is only necessary to go back to the coupling rod problem. Even if the method outlined above has been carefully carried out and everything is perfect except that one crank pin is out of square, then the coupling rods will still not fit correctly and it would be useless making an 'out of square' bush to suit the faulty pin – that would only make matters worse. The only remedy would be to bore out the offending hole in correct alignment and make and fit a new pin.

The idea behind describing the process in this chapter has been to illustrate once again that the method of manufacture, particularly of components that form part of an assembly, can influence not only the measuring techniques involved but also the ease with which the assembly can be produced and the degree of success obtained in the working of the finished unit. It pays therefore not to rush into the construction but rather to carefully plan the methods to be used and the sequence of the operations to be followed. The method chosen for any given exercise will naturally depend on the equipment available and also on the experience of the operator. Do not be put off by lack of experience: if you have an idea 'have a go', if the idea works then great satisfaction is gained, if not, you have at least added to your experience and the old saying quotes that "experience is cheap at any price"!